SELF-COACHING
THE DRAGON WITHIN

The hardest person you'll ever lead is you

KELLIE GARRETT

Self-Coaching the Dragon Within

2024 fEMPOWER Press Trade Paperback Edition.
Copyright © 2024 Kellie Garrett

All Rights Reserved. No part of this book can be scanned, distributed, or copied without permission. This book or any portion thereof may not be reproduced or used in any manner whatsoever without the express written permission of the publisher at sabrina@fempower.pub —except for the use of brief quotations in a book review.

The author has made every effort to ensure the accuracy of the information within this book was correct at time of publication. The author does not assume and hereby disclaims any liability to any party for any loss, damage, or disruption caused by errors or omissions, whether such errors or omissions result from accident, negligence, or any other cause. Some names and identifying details have been changed to protect the privacy of those discussed.

This book is not intended to be a substitute for the medical advice of a licensed physician. The reader should consult with their doctor in any matters relating to their health.

All images and supporting information used with permission.

The publisher is not responsible for websites (or their content) that are not owned by the publisher.

Published in Canada, for Global Distribution
by fEMPOWER Publications Inc.
www.fempower.pub
For more information email: sabrina@fempower.pub

ISBN trade paperback: 978-1-998754-71-7
eBook: 978-1-998754-72-4

To order additional copies of this book:
sabrina@fempower.pub

*People who deny
the existence of dragons
are often eaten by dragons.
From within.*

–Ursula K. Le Guin

TRIGGER WARNING

IMPORTANT:

Do not coach yourself if you have mental health issues or PTSD, or experience anxiety or other issues. See a certified counselor.

Coaching (including self-coaching) cannot take the place of counseling.

Look after yourself.

"Leadership mastery is inseparable from personal transformation, which requires moving from one stage of consciousness to the next. This requires acknowledging your light and courageously embracing your shadow (what Kellie calls dragons). This book will help you explore both so you can fully shine your light and inspire others to do the same. The world needs all of us to do just that."

–Bob Anderson, Founder & Chairman,
The Leadership Circle™

ACKNOWLEDGMENTS

This was going to be short, but I have a need to include everyone. ☺

- My darling grown men. Learning how to be your mother made me a better human. Jay and I are so proud of you, and your dad was too:

  · Max: I appreciate your kindness, humor, loyalty, and questing spirit. You are so special.

  · Connor: You defied the dire predictions that came with the autism diagnosis and didn't let it define you. You are so happy in your skin. Yay for you!

- My soulmate and husband, Jay Henryk—my partner in life and one of my best coaches. Your love, intelligence, depth, and passion sustain me. You are my favorite earthly joy. (Which says a lot because you know how much I love gardening!) ♥

- My talented sister, Robin Garrett—yogini, hiking leader, chef, tea aficionado, wondrous mom, and former CEO. You have cheered me on in every area of my life since you were born. Dearest Robin, your "heaps" of love mean the world to me.

- Brenda Garrett (née Barrett): My brilliant, mystical, artistic, thought-provoking mother. You thought I'd publish a book by age thirty. I finally did it. Miss your one-of-a-kind self thirty-four years after losing you.

- Walter Garrett: My funny, nature-loving, kind, gardener-extraordinaire father. I carry your last words, "love you up," in my heart.

- My kindred spirits: You know who you are. Thank you for the laughter, escapades, soul-searching, and support.

- My wonderful groups: such sources of fun and sparkling conversation—BOHOs, Liver Die, Philosophers, and Quest.

On the work front, a huge thank you to:

- Former FCC Chief Operating Officer and fiercely bright Louise Neveu, who saw potential in me before I did and gave me a promotion before I felt ready. Her tough-love approach was rocket fuel for my subsequent career success. (And she wore kick-ass clothes.) Louise, I'm forever grateful. And happy you're a kindred spirit friend. ☺

- Former FCC CEO John Ryan, who kept throwing new challenges at me, including running for his job. Whenever I protested, he'd say, "Do you trust me?" I did, so he always won. John, thank you for believing in me.

- Former FCC CEO Greg Stewart, who supported me through my prickliness after I lost the CEO race. Greg, thank you for convincing me to stay on as your wing woman. I learned such humility during that time and came to genuinely support your leadership.

- Retired EVP & CHRO Greg Honey, who masterminded FCC's amazing journey to #5 on Canada's Top 50 Employers' list. I learned so much from your passion to create organizational cultures that bring out people's potential. Our lifelong bond began when we became certified coaches together and grows ever stronger.

- My first great boss, Jodi Macpherson, who modeled laser focus and taught that it was okay to weave warmth into relationships with employees.

- Pam McLean, CEO & Cofounder of the Hudson Institute of Coaching: your wisdom—about coaching and all things human development—is unparalleled. Thank you for pushing me to go well beyond the questions as a coach.

- Masterful coach, leadership expert, and dear friend Susan Mann, who convinced me to become a Dare to Lead™ Facilitator. Can't wait for our next art trip!

- Brené Brown, with whom I had the privilege of meeting along with fourteen other Dare to Lead Facilitators for a full day. Your work is inspirational and life-changing for many reasons, including a sense that every fiber of your being is committed to making a difference in the world.

- My coaching clients and former colleagues: I learned more from you than you'll ever know.

On the quest to be a better leader and human, thank you to:

- My wonderful coaches: Tracey Burns, Marlene Clark, Sue Cruse, Chris Dierkes, John Doan, Tana Heminsley, Maggie Larkin, Dr. Jay Lewis, and Jodi Woollam. You helped me face down my dragons so I could shine.

- Bob Anderson, the brilliant creator of the Leadership Circle: Training with you was transformational. You looked at my 360 and said it was time to let go of constant self-criticism, training, and self-improvement. When you gazed at me with your big compassionate eyes and said, "Step into the mystical and *be* radiance," it was a jolt of awakening.

My writing wizards:

- Writing coach and hilarious, passionate Tina Overbury, who wrangled the beginning bones of this book out of me, and Maribeth Jasmine Deen's whip-smart mind and keen insights (thanks for the Ursula K. Le Guin quote ☺). The Joshua Tree writing retreat with you two fired up my muse.

- Editor Christine Stock, who resolutely pushed me to take this book to a new level. It is much better because of you.

- Writing coach Anna Sonser, who gave me the magic ingredients to finally birth this book. I cannot thank you enough.

- The great peeps at Soul Seed Legacy Publishing: you brought my dream to life.

Finally, thank you to my trio of dragons: Gusto, Never Enough, and Perfecto. I set out to slay you. Instead, I embraced your teachings and gently pushed you off center stage.

TABLE OF CONTENTS

Acknowledgments vi
How to Read This Book 01
Prologue: This Is Your Higher Self Speaking 03
Introduction 06

Part I – Leadership, Consciousness, and Your Higher Self 15
Chapter 1: Leadership as a Way of Being 16
Chapter 2: Leadership and Levels of Consciousness 29
Chapter 3: Your Higher Self 49

Part II – The Dragon Within 71
Chapter 4: Dueling with Dragons – My Story 72
Chapter 5: Brené Brown and the Mother of All Dragons: Shame .89
Chapter 6: Finding Your Dragon Within 101

Part III – Common Coaching Issues 111
Chapter 7: Top Coaching Themes 112
Chapter 8: Coaching Issue – Emotional Intelligence 115
Chapter 9: Coaching Issue – Trust 132
Chapter 10: Coaching Issue – Confidence 149
Chapter 11: Coaching Issue – Mental Toughness 158
Chapter 12: Coaching Issue – Political Savvy and Power 167
Chapter 13: Coaching Issue – Feedback 176

Part IV – The Coaching Process and Self-Coaching with the DRAGONS Model.................191

Chapter 14: Jolts of Awakening – The Coaching Process........192
Chapter 15: Self-Coaching Checklist.................200
Chapter 16: DRAGONS Self-Coaching Model.................212
DRAGONS Self-Coaching Example.................219

Part V – The Journey to Mastery.................229

Chapter 17: Self-Mastery and Transcendence.................230
Epilogue: This is Your Higher Self Speaking.................238

Part VI – Integrating Your Learnings.................241

My Learning Integration Plan.................242

APPENDIX.................246

Additional Coaching Questions.................246
Additional Ideas to Access Your Higher Self.................254
End Notes.................256
Author Bio.................260

HOW TO READ THIS BOOK

My goal is to provide you with practical ways to coach yourself—into leadership as a way of being that permeates your whole life.

Part I discusses leadership as a way of being, its link to elevated consciousness, and enlisting your higher self as a wise inner guide.

Part II is all about the dragon within: my story and a chapter devoted to helping you discover your dragons.

Part III shares common coaching issues. You may find one to use in your self-coaching.

Part IV discusses the process used by professional coaches as the basis of self-coaching and introduces the DRAGONS self-coaching model.

Part V shares thoughts on the journey to self-mastery and challenges you to demonstrate leadership as a way of being that's connected to your level of consciousness.

Part VI provides a template to integrate your learnings from the book and move forward with an action plan.

The Appendix contains additional coaching questions and practices to access your higher self.

- At the end of every chapter, you'll find a workbook with questions and short exercises to apply the content. You can complete them as you progress through the book. If you're like me, you'll skim them and complete them later.

- Choose a journal devoted to self-coaching where you can write your answers to the workbook sections. You can leave blank journal pages after each section to journal about what you notice as you apply the learnings. If you're not into pen and paper, use an online journal.

- At the end of the book, you'll find an integration plan to knit together your learnings. You'll emerge with a go-forward plan to confidently coach yourself. Again, you can complete this right away or sit with what you've learned for a while before you tackle it.

There's no right or wrong way.
You do you.

You can access more helpful tools,
including a DRAGONS self-coaching template,
on my website **kelliegarrett.ca** with this code:

You can also join the Facebook group Self-Coaching the Dragon Within at https://www.facebook.com/groups/3647301828914144

PROLOGUE – THIS IS YOUR HIGHER SELF SPEAKING

This is your higher self speaking. So far, I've heard you fretting about getting home late again, being short with the kids, wondering why your boss is avoiding you, resenting your colleague's end run, and thinking you should return your friend's call. You beat yourself up about choosing sloth instead of exercise and drinking too much wine last night. You're exhausted, and so is your husband. The dark circles under his eyes are worse than yours. You didn't ask about it, wanting to avoid criticism from him about not pulling your weight. And all this happened in just the last twenty minutes.

Your inner dragons are running the show. What are dragons? They're a mixture of your inner critic, limiting beliefs about who you're supposed to be, and protective behaviors. This dark triad has taken over. You have so much light inside, but it's currently smothered. All those stories about who you are? All that stuff that's troubling you? Lots of it isn't true or important. Most isn't in sync with your soul, let alone feeding it. What if you just . . . stopped? Tuned into me?

If you had a coach who sat in complete non-judgment, what would you talk about? Would you pour out everything you long for in life—at home and at work? Your fears and inadequacies? Pretend I'm her. Pretend until you see that I *am* her.

It's time to ditch what isn't serving you. Stop looking outside yourself for answers. Stop zipping between beating yourself up and blaming others when things upset you. There's a still, safe place inside you that knows how amazing you are. Amazing isn't the same as perfect. That place also knows exactly where you need to pull up your socks, even if you're fuzzy about it.

This is your higher self. I'm not God, I'm not perfect, and I'm not woo-woo. Some people call me the soul. Others call me essence. I'm at your core. No matter what you're ashamed of, what you wish you hadn't done, what you worry about, what you never get right, I'm always here. I can serve as a steady compass—your guide inside. You lose sight of me when you're racing around or numbing yourself with social media, wine, and overwork. You forget that I am YOU, the real you. I'm the one who can help you to consistently show up the way you want to. Or, more accurately, to tap into **being** who you already are. You just need to reintegrate your everyday self with me, your higher self. Easier said than done, I know.

If I were your executive coach, I'd ask you questions, starting with what you'd like to achieve by the end of your coaching program. What's serving you about how you are living? What isn't? What thought patterns are helpful? Which ones drag you down? What disturbs your inner peace? Who do you wish you could be? How do you want to react when things go off the rails? What inner dragons claw at your sense of worth? What are your towering strengths and crippling flaws? Are they somehow related to each other? (Spoiler alert: yes, they are.)

You are the CEO of your own life. CEOs understand the ins and outs of leadership, which starts with self-awareness and its pesky cousin, self-management: managing your reactions and your interactions. Great leaders listen to their inner critic's voices with curiosity, not attachment. They tune into their higher self and courageously follow its wisdom. CEOs engage coaches to challenge and support them. Adopt a CEO mindset.

Our coaching engagement can last a lifetime. Hire your higher self. For you, a special price: I'm free. And I'm waiting.

> "USE THE LIGHT THAT DWELLS WITHIN YOU
> TO REGAIN YOUR NATURAL CLARITY OF SIGHT."
> –Lao Tzu

INTRODUCTION

I'm a recovering executive and graduate from the School of Overdoing, whose subjects included overthinking, workaholism, perfectionism, and deriving self-worth from accomplishments. Many coaches helped enhance my leadership. This transformed how I live my life. Leadership is far more about a way of being than it is about vision, goal setting, and technical know-how. The lion's share of leadership is about human connection. How we **be** in relationship with others can only be as healthy as our relationship with ourselves.

In my case, the triple crown of talent, work ethic, and playing well with others rocketed me up the ranks in my midthirties. I wasn't ready. This sparked credential-seeking behavior to prove I was good enough: from a graduate degree in leadership to certification in executive coaching. I also participated in several leadership development programs. Self-awareness is the bedrock of such programs. Observing similar relationship patterns with two husbands also provided valuable, if annoying, insights. Oh, and there was individual and marriage therapy too. (Brené Brown says she's never met a great leader who hasn't had a coach, a therapist, or both. Yay me.) I learned from great bosses along the way and a few soul-destroying ones. Parenting provided many lessons, including how to navigate joint custody and autism challenges.

I was lucky enough to receive executive coaching in my forties and benefited greatly. My talented coaches helped me uncover limiting beliefs, a host of inner critics, and protective behaviors that weren't serving me. I call this dark triad "dragons." They sent me messages like . . .

> *You're not good enough.*
> *You're too sensitive.*
> *You don't belong.*
> *You want too much.*
> *You're too idealistic.*
> *You're too much for people.*

It felt like my own voice, when really, it was dragons masquerading as me. The statements felt like truths and drove many of my feelings and behaviors. Maggie Larkin, my first coach, held up the mirror, asked provocative questions, and helped me dramatically increase self-awareness, much more than all the training had. I started noticing my reactions and patterns everywhere. It was wildly uncomfortable.

Every meeting with my coach was a haven. I could vent, cry, and share what wasn't working. I never felt judged or like a lost cause. Each coach listened, asked provocative questions, and gave me ideas to try out when I was stuck. They helped me embrace everything about myself, including what I don't like. I learned more self-compassion, which expanded compassion for others. I finally acknowledged my powerful presence. I couldn't see it because I felt warm and flawed. How could that be intimidating? But perception is reality. I took accountability for my impact (that sounds buzzwordy, but it's true). At first, I overcompensated, showing up quiet and reserved. People wondered what the hell was going on with me. Gradually, I found a way to be myself without taking up all the air in the room. Like magic, relationships with colleagues improved dramatically.

The growth that occurred was phenomenal. I became a much better leader at work and a better human in general.

Daring to look within

Long after the coaches had departed, my continued transformation relied on coaching myself. This entailed five things:

1. Viewing leadership as a way of being

My heart always knew that leadership is a way of being that isn't tied to title. This was brought home fully while serving in various executive positions, serving on boards, and learning in academic settings, including Harvard Business School. I became fascinated by how many people had titles but didn't demonstrate leadership behaviors. I started seeing where I was "being" a leader and where I wasn't. I became committed to demonstrating leadership at work and in my personal life, and inspiring others to do the same.

2. Learning about vertical development and consciousness growth

When I found that our level of consciousness drives our way of being, I learned about vertical development (covered in Chapter 2). This entails growth in maturity and wisdom, expanding our perspective, and increasing our concern for others—at work and elsewhere. This helps us to better navigate complexity and ambiguity, and deal with paradox, which allows more openness to other viewpoints.

3. Tuning into my higher self

Deeply listening to the core of myself (my soul or essence) serves as a wonderful inner compass. I call this my higher self. When connected, I feel complete self-acceptance. The dragons don't get any oxygen. This allows me to notice and correct the stories I tell myself. I grant myself grace and extend it to others. When tuned into my higher self, I discern what's right for me. Now and then, I pose questions. Sometimes I hear the answer right away. But in many instances, I simply sit with the question. I walk, shower, write, and meditate on it. And eventually, I experience a deep knowing. That's why I've enlisted my higher self as my self-coaching wing woman.

You find what's deeply true for you when you're integrated with your higher self. What ways of being detract from who you really are? What ways make you feel expansive and aware? Seeking more and more ways to live in sync is the goal here.

Now, if this is too woo-woo for you, replace the concept of your higher self with your soul. What is the call of your soul? What feeds it and drags it down? Use what works for you. The point is to get out of your overthinking head and tune into what's deep within you. That inner depth IS you.

4. Using a coaching process

Coaches start by asking your goals: What do you want to be different after the coaching is over? Then you dive into your current reality, unpack behavior patterns, hopefully have an aha or two, try new things, and determine a way forward: practices and actions to embed what you've learned and sustain it. (This makes it sound easy; it's not.) I adapted these steps to develop my own coaching process, which I called DRAGONS. I use it for issues big and small.

5. Feedback from others

You can't coach yourself in a vacuum. (Well, you can, but it won't be effective.) Once I knew that my higher self loved and accepted me exactly as I was, receiving feedback became much easier. My curious self learned to solicit feedback everywhere: at work, at home, on boards, and even with friends. Just like with the 360s I received on the job, themes inevitably show up. I sift through the themes when I coach myself.

Facing the dragon within

Becoming a coach myself was illuminating. I've been struck by the pervasive presence of a powerful inner critic, accompanied by limiting beliefs and protective behaviors. I call this combination the dragon within. Some of my dragons clawed at my very soul. Once I identified the dragons, I could experiment with different ways of dealing with them, some more effective than others. Although I couldn't annihilate them (very disappointing), they no longer run the show. This process opened me up to a new way of being: living my life in sync with my higher self—who I really am at my core.

As a coach, I discovered that I wasn't the only high-achieving executive with dragons. After hundreds of coaching hours, two major themes emerged with respect to what clients needed to learn or unlearn:

1. Self-awareness and a need to regulate reactions:
- Big inner critics that erode confidence and fuel the impostor syndrome
- Limiting beliefs
- Arrogance and lack of self-awareness
- Not managing reactions well (even if it's not evident to others)

2. Interpersonal relationships:
- Listening, empathy, giving and receiving feedback, and discomfort with politics and power
- Controlling or people-pleasing behaviors
- Over-reliance on relationships to the detriment of results and accountability
- Driving for results at the expense of relationships

While every client is unique, most coaching issues boil down to the above: the inner and outer game of leadership—managing yourself in relationship with others and your own self. And a dragon is usually at the root, preventing progress. Is it really that simple? I've concluded the answer is yes. But simple doesn't mean easy.

If you truly want to positively impact others—as a leader, parent, spouse, friend, or volunteer—you need to look within. Who are you at your core? Where are your actions in sync with your authentic, higher self? Do you have the courage to face where you need to change? If you do, you'll be astonished at how much better your life will be. This way of being won't eradicate all your problems. But you'll feel more equipped to deal with them.

In many ways, leadership is akin to a spiritual journey. It's simultaneously all about you—your reactions, patterns, blind spots, passions, selfish moments—and not about you at all. It's a dance between self-awareness and managing yourself in relationship with others. Choosing leadership in every area of your life will transform how you process emotions, the thoughts in your head, relationships, and how you "be" everywhere.

You take your real self to work, to your relationships, to your kid's tantrums, to dinner parties. If you don't know who your real self is, or you don't like him/her/them, you'll try to stuff yourself down. But who we really are always has a way of showing up, often at inconvenient times.

I think the world needs more people who choose leadership, day in and day out. If a critical mass of people chose to interact from a leadership stance, I imagine diminished political games in organizations, less vitriol on social media, and fewer battles about children after divorce. Some people attain this way of being with zero access to leadership training or coaches. Most of us could use a little help.

Few of us are lucky enough to have a trusted coach to help sift through our current state and define what we want to change. My coaches helped me see that my resistance to embracing who I really was—including my shadow side—was blocking my quest to be a highly conscious leader.

Because I'm driven to help others shine, I wrote this book to share my aha's. I really love aha's. One coach told me that my wonderful aha's weren't producing behavior change. True. But they do spark the awareness required to get somewhere. When something catapults you to a new level of consciousness, a new way of thinking and being, you just sit in wonder. Why couldn't I see what's so clear now? What else am I not seeing?

I get a jolt of joy whenever I help others discover their own aha's. My wish is to help you uncover yours so that you can deal with your own inner dragons (or stop letting the stubborn ones hog the spotlight) so you can realize your potential and follow your leadership path. Ideally, you'll feel moved to help others shine too. Hopefully, you'll move closer to inner peace, which in my opinion, is the best and only measure of success.

My leadership journey has left me with this:
- a deep desire to continue moving to a higher level of consciousness—not just when I feel Zen, but especially

- when I'm frustrated or hurt, critical, triggered, or tired (or hangry).
- the knowledge that some dragons simply can't be slayed (sigh). When they roar into view, I have coping techniques to prevent them from derailing me from living in sync with my values and my higher self.
- a passion for helping everyone feel seen, that they matter, and realize their struggles, desires, and sorrows are necessary to access inner growth.
- a zeal to help people access more success (whatever they conceive that to be) by paradoxically owning how they get in their own way.
- a quest to help encourage as many people as possible to step into their potential and feel moved to help others do the same.

This book is designed to help you embody leadership as a way of being, grow your level of consciousness, and connect with your higher self. My goal is to help you deal with what's not serving you by using the DRAGONS self-coaching model.

What is your leadership journey trying to teach you? May this book help you find your way.

The hardest person you'll ever lead is you.

> "WHERE WE HAD THOUGHT TO SLAY ANOTHER, WE SHALL SLAY OURSELVES. WHERE WE HAD THOUGHT TO TRAVEL OUTWARD, WE WILL COME TO THE CENTER OF OUR OWN EXISTENCE."
>
> –Joseph Campbell, *The Power of Myth*

PART I

LEADERSHIP, CONSCIOUSNESS, AND YOUR HIGHER SELF

CHAPTER 1: LEADERSHIP AS A WAY OF BEING

The goal of this chapter is to convey that leadership is a way of being that isn't tied to title. How you "be" at work and elsewhere in life reflects your level of consciousness. Are you all about you? Or does the person in front of you matter to the point where you become more interested in helping them shine than shining a light on yourself? Do you keep the organization as a whole top of mind or fight for your silo? And in your personal life, do you rise above irritations and do what's right for your child, your ex, your community? That's leadership.

"LEADERSHIP IS A WAY OF BEING; IT'S A WAY OF LIFE."
–Nozomi Morgan, coach and leadership consultant

"How come you don't give other people your homework?" asked my eight-year-old.

"What do you mean?" I asked.

"Well, aren't you a triple boss?"

"Huh?"

"A boss that has a boss that has a boss that has you as the big boss."

"I guess so." How did he know this?

"Then why are you doing all the work?" (Out of the mouths of babes . . .)

"Because bosses have to do work too," I explained. Max looked at me funny.

"Hmm. Maybe you're not a real leader then. Bosses are supposed to boss people. Moms do that too, and you're good at bossing us around. And are you paying attention when you're at work? 'Cause you're always telling me I'll have less homework if I concentrate." I laughed. Maybe not.

"I concentrate as hard as I can, but I get a lot of interruptions. People want to talk to me."

"Mom, I do too, but I just tell them we can't talk or we'll get in trouble. And I tell my brain to stay on task. Maybe you should try that."

My kid thought leadership meant bossing people around. While it's tempting some days to just dictate what everyone should do, that's not leadership. Humans don't like being told what to do. "You're not the boss of me" starts at two years old and never really goes away. Being a true leader is about choosing leadership regardless of circumstance, not just at work but everywhere else. I don't know about you but being my own boss hasn't been a cakewalk. Hence the subtitle: *The hardest person you'll ever lead is you.*

Unfortunately, there are many lousy bosses out there who wouldn't know good leadership if it hit them. Everyone has had crappy managers. My first soul-destroying one was fired after a class action suit for bullying and harassment. She drove me from a job I loved when I was twenty-nine. The silver lining was finding new work under an amazing leader, Jodi Macpherson. I was fascinated by the difference. Why did Jodi warmly treat us like intelligent individuals, which unleashed our energy and led to great results? Why do other bosses like to step on people?

You can have a boss title and never show up as a leader. You can work in the print shop, with no education and no direct reports, and act like a leader every day. I've met special education teachers who quietly help children reach their potential. I've seen social workers with crushing caseloads give us their full attention. Parents who don't criticize their ex in front of their kids are choosing leadership, as are children when they stand up to bullies.

At work, leadership behaviors include collaboration, openness to others' views, and genuinely being curious about how you can improve. It means simultaneously showing compassion and making sure results happen. Prickly peers need to be handled without criticizing them behind their backs. (That used to be a bad habit of mine if I thought they deserved it. Not good.) In your personal life, do you demonstrate leadership behaviors? Treat your partner like . . . a partner? Listen to your kids with curiosity more than judgment? Collaborate with your ex on childcare and say kind things about them to your children? Support your friends and refrain from gossip? Do you grant others grace when they screw up?

The hardest person you'll ever lead is you

Leadership means being the boss of you—at work and everywhere else. Leading yourself requires awareness of your strengths and how they become flaws when overplayed. It involves understanding your default responses and motivations. It's recognizing that relationships and *how* you do things always override *what* you do—at work and elsewhere. Achieving results at the expense of others isn't sustainable. If you're in management, choosing leadership behavior allows you to inspire your teams to achieve goals and provide feedback that motivates instead of crushes. Apologizing for your mistakes or negative impact models vulnerability and encourages others to follow suit.

Being the boss of you on the personal front means managing your reactions and being genuinely interested in others' needs: your spouse, kids, friends, and even your ex. Choosing leadership behaviors fosters true connection.

Choosing leadership requires a willingness to face your shadow side. Psychologist Carl Jung described the shadow as parts of yourself that you find unpleasant and repress because they contradict what you like about yourself. Jung called them shadows because you can't see them clearly and don't want to—it's too painful.[1]

I call our shadow side dragons—a combo pack of what you don't like about yourself as well as your harsh inner critic, limiting beliefs, and protective behaviors. It's easier to avoid thinking about any of this. But Jung wisely said, "What you resist persists and grows in size." Allowing yourself to truly feel discomfort and even pain is the first step to addressing how you're getting in your own way and negatively impacting others. You can't manage what you don't acknowledge.

Know thyself: The foundation of leadership

Leadership programs emphasize emotional intelligence (EI), which is rooted in self-awareness. Understanding your emotions and go-to reactions are key to managing yourself in relationship with others. This helps you match your intentions with your desired impact. Emotional intelligence is also about detecting where others are at and engaging from a stance of "we" rather than "me." I thought I was an EI rock star. After all, I was in touch with my feelings and had pretty accurate radar about other people's emotions. But when it came to self-regulation, I had a hard time getting unhooked when triggered.

How hard can it be to align your behaviors with who you want to be? Or better said, who you really are at your core? It's tougher for some of us than others. What got you promoted often doesn't work in the long run. Aligning your best self with how you show up requires accepting everything about yourself. "Everything" includes what you don't like. This means the courage to face down your dragons and recognize how you sabotage yourself. It's work at a deep soul level. And it will rock what you know about yourself, right down to your identity. It's counterintuitive, but you'll obtain more clarity when you stop believing you have everything figured out.

Leadership as a behavior is all about paradox. It's like Goldilocks: the porridge is rarely the right temperature:

- It's all about you—how well you know yourself. Tuned into who you really are, aware of your strengths/flaws,

default reactions, motivations. At the same time, it's all about others: tuned into where they're at, managing yourself in relationship with them.
- Self-compassion when you screw up and compassion for others when they do.
- Sensitivity: feeling deeply is a strength; too much can become neurotic.
- Mental toughness: pushing through difficulty is a strength; too much can result in lack of empathy.
- Boundaries are great when they aren't brick walls.
- Trying hard things versus staying safe and expecting others to act first.
- Knowing when to just listen and not offer any advice when you're bursting to give it.
- Using a coach approach at the very same time you're holding someone accountable.
- Showing empathy when you're frustrated that a peer has missed another deadline, while still holding them accountable.
- Leadership is both a grind and an uplifting pursuit. It's hard work and easier to phone it in. It's uplifting because all is well with your soul when you choose leadership behaviors and help others do the same.

To make progress, you need to hold these and other polarities in your mind, knowing both are true. I am wonderful and operate in sync with my higher self and sometimes awful, ruled by my small self, on the same day. Until you recognize your part to play in challenges (even if your ability to control what's going on is limited), your dragons run the show. Once you accept each dragon's presence, you can examine them. How have they served you? How are they hindering you? Is it time to get rid of some? Or train them, like the movie my kid loved? No matter how hard you try, some dragons simply can't be eradicated. Instead, befriend them. Whether you slay them or not, they have much to teach you—powerful lessons that apply at work and elsewhere in life. This is necessary to live up to yourself—to be who you say you want to be. Your dragons stand in your way. Having the courage to face them down is a hard and fascinating journey. You'll still have flaws and screw up (sorry). But the magic of transformation only works when you stop externalizing blame *and* stop internalizing (thinking it's all your fault.) Embracing your shadow lessens its grip.

Bringing out the best in others starts with you

In her marvelous book *Self as Coach, Self as Leader*, Pamela McLean focuses on the power of the "use of self" as a leader and coach. (McLean is the chair and cofounder of the Hudson Institute of Coaching, my alma mater.) She identifies the following areas to enhance the use of self: presence, empathy, range of feelings, boundaries, embodiment (centering ourselves in the body) and courage (willingness to be candid and share provocative insights).

The world needs you to choose self-leadership. We need this at work, at home with partners and family, in our communities, and working for causes. This isn't about perfection. People who demonstrate leadership behaviors are real and flawed. They do their inner work, manage their reactions, and clean up after adversely impacting people. And they do this, over and over, even if no one around them seems to be.

When you realize that everyone is flawed, you can quit pretending you're perfect and stop expecting it of others. You can hold accountability conversations with compassion. The best leaders know that creating other great leaders is the goal. They're more consumed with developing those around them than shining a light on themselves. Too many people are so intent on personal success that they begrudge others the time and space to grow. But before you can bring out the best in others, you must bring out the best in yourself. You need to know where your talents and flaws lie, with a clear and objective eye. If you want to succeed, you must feel what that means to you personally—at a soul level, personally and professionally—untainted by other people's definition of success.

When you conquer your dragons (or at least manage them), you can truly lead yourself, a precursor to leading anyone else. It's difficult to accept that you can't eliminate all dragons. Isn't there a hack for that? No. Some things are embedded so deep, the best you can do is diminish their power. You need to stop equating the dragon with who you really are. It's not some deep internal flaw. Dragons often develop as a protective mechanism. Later, they outlive their usefulness.

Realizing your potential isn't all about mystical aha's. Some parts are hard and boring. It requires energy that's not easy to sustain. The tough grunt work of leading yourself is a prerequisite to leading others. You owe it to them. As former FCC CEO Greg Stewart used to say, "Everyone deserves a good leader." Leadership is a choice, every single day. We choose to expand our concerns beyond ourselves. We regulate our emotions and manage our reactions. We choose to be curious more than directive.

Retired Chief HR Officer Greg Honey masterminded FCC's culture transformation, which led to a #5 spot on Canada's Top 50 Employers list. He says, "As leaders, we make many choices every day. One choice CANNOT be whether I care for someone or not. It comes with the territory: you must love your employees. Every single one. The ones we have the most to learn from are those we find the most difficult. Those colleagues and team members we think (maybe) we don't care for. **Caring is not optional. You don't get to NOT care.**"

On particularly challenging days, it won't feel worth it. You just won't care. You'll justify your annoyances. You'll avoid or criticize colleagues. That's okay. You're human, dammit. You get to start again, over and over. Eventually, your small self will overshadow your higher self less. You'll see your dragons and they won't hold you hostage. You'll care deeply for everyone around you. You'll exude leadership as a way of being and inspire others to do the same, regardless of title.

The hardest person you'll ever lead is you. I know you have it in you to succeed.

*"IN OJIBWE AND CREE CULTURE,
'LEADERSHIP' DIDN'T MEAN POWER, IT MEANT CARING."*
–Tanya Talaga, author and visionary for Canada's reconciliation journey

KELLIE GARRETT

CHAPTER 1 WORKBOOK

ELECTRONIC VERSIONS OF ALL WORKBOOKS ARE AVAILABLE AT KELLIEGARRETT.CA

What does leadership mean to me?

If leadership is a way of being, I think the associated leadership behaviors are _____ . (List as many as you like.)

Which of these leadership behaviors do I consistently demonstrate?

At work:

In my personal life:

What leadership behaviors do I want to demonstrate more?

At work:

In my personal life:

What gets in the way of demonstrating these behaviors?

At work:

In my personal life:

What would help me consistently demonstrate these behaviors?

At work:

In my personal life:

Would facing my dragons (what I repress and don't like about myself, my inner critic, my limiting beliefs, and my protective behaviors) help me demonstrate leadership as a way of being?

My takeaways after completing this exercise:

Resources

Self as Coach, Self as Leader, Pamela McLean, chair and cofounder, The Hudson Institute of Coaching.

There are free worksheets on Hudson's website: https://hudsoninstitute.com/self-as-coach/self-as-coach-model/

CHAPTER 2: LEADERSHIP AND LEVELS OF CONSCIOUSNESS

Leadership is a way of being driven by your level of consciousness. This chapter discusses how these important topics are intertwined. You can choose to question the lens through which you view the world and elevate your consciousness. This will dramatically affect how you "be" as a leader.

"We often describe unconscious leaders as reactive. They react from a 'story' about the past or an imagined future, and their personality, ego, or mind takes over."[2]

After growing up in a somewhat dysfunctional home, I vowed to be highly functional: a higher consciousness rock star. I'd be positive in every situation, and exude warmth, kindness, and compassion—always. Being human, this obviously didn't happen. I beat myself up after any transgression, comparing myself against my perfectionistic standards. One of my friends asked, "Who do you think you are? Jesus? Buddha? You're human, y'know." I did know but still dreamed of what I could be, should be. I remember reading a sentence on a CD that instantly resonated: "Keep pure your highest ideal; strive ever toward it; let naught stop you or turn you aside."[3] I eventually wove it into what I thought of as my life quest: *To strive ever toward my highest ideal, making the world a better place with every word and action.*

The only problem was its impossibility. Nobody's perfect. I set myself up, birthing a ferocious dragon I called Perfecto-Bun. My budding knowledge about consciousness fueled this dragon. If there were seven levels of consciousness, I wanted to be at seven. If there were 10, I'd go for 9.5. (Kinda like figure skating in the Olympics. I imagined an unseen force holding up a sign with my score.) I completely missed the point. A focus on my highest ideals promoted all-or-nothing thinking. It blinded me to where I really was on the consciousness scale. I swung between self-satisfaction and self-flagellation. I am wise and highly conscious (self-satisfaction). I am an amazing listener (yay!). Yelling at my kids or criticizing colleagues (yikes!). Agonizing over my divorce, yet again (sigh).

Along the way, I read extensively on higher consciousness. I knew lots *about* consciousness. But I hadn't integrated the learning. Knowing and being are different. I continued to equate advanced consciousness with having no dark side (being perfect). I didn't understand that those who ascend to more elevated levels completely embrace their flaws and their gifts (they're often two sides of the same coin).

Leadership and consciousness

It sounds obvious, but if you want to behave like a leader, you need to learn how to lead *you*. This requires self-awareness, which helps you understand your mindset, go-to emotions, habitual reactions, how you act when things go wrong, and everything else about how you *be*. This benefits you and everyone around you because operating at higher levels of consciousness is highly correlated with leadership effectiveness.[4] As management guru Peter Drucker said, "Your foremost job as a leader is to take care of your own emotional energy and then help orchestrate the energy of those around you." This is vitally important if you wish to manifest leadership as a way of being at work and everywhere else in life, whether you're a manager or not.

Tending to your way of being involves deep work. As a young man, Leadership Circle founder Bob Anderson became fascinated by how people develop from the inside out. He decided his life's work was to help people grow and develop emotionally, psychologically, and spiritually. He was exposed to many thought leaders, including Robert Kegan (adult development), Carl Jung (ego/shadow), and Peter Senge (systems thinking). As Anderson pondered their theories and frameworks, he noticed they weren't connected. He set about integrating theories from leadership, psychology, consciousness, spirituality, and human potential.[5] The result was his Universal Model of Leadership. He mapped several of the levels to Kegan's adult development theory. Kegan believed that there are three possible levels we can grow into once we leave the egocentric ways of childhood and adolescence:[6]

Socialized mind – I am what others think

At this level, you define yourself by those around you. Your beliefs and what you value are subject to what others believe and value. It's like you're looking at everything through the lenses of others and making choices accordingly.

Self-authoring mind – this is what I think

You decide what you believe for yourself, who you are, and how you want to be in relationship with others. You aren't subject to what others think or believe; that is, your worth is not in others' hands.

Self-transforming mind – how else can it be understood?

You can go beyond your beliefs, ideas, and behaviors and critically examine them. What lens are you using to look at the world? You can change what you examine and transcend your limitations. You're better at seeing shades of gray, can embrace paradox and criticize yourself without attachment. This makes you open to feedback from others with curiosity and without defensiveness.

Anderson's Universal Model of Leadership illustrates leadership as a way of being. At each level, your identity drives your sense of yourself and informs how you see the world. Progressive levels of consciousness involve restructuring your identity as you move from self-centeredness to more concern for others. Each stage allows you to embrace increasingly complex meaning-making systems.

Universal Model of Leadership

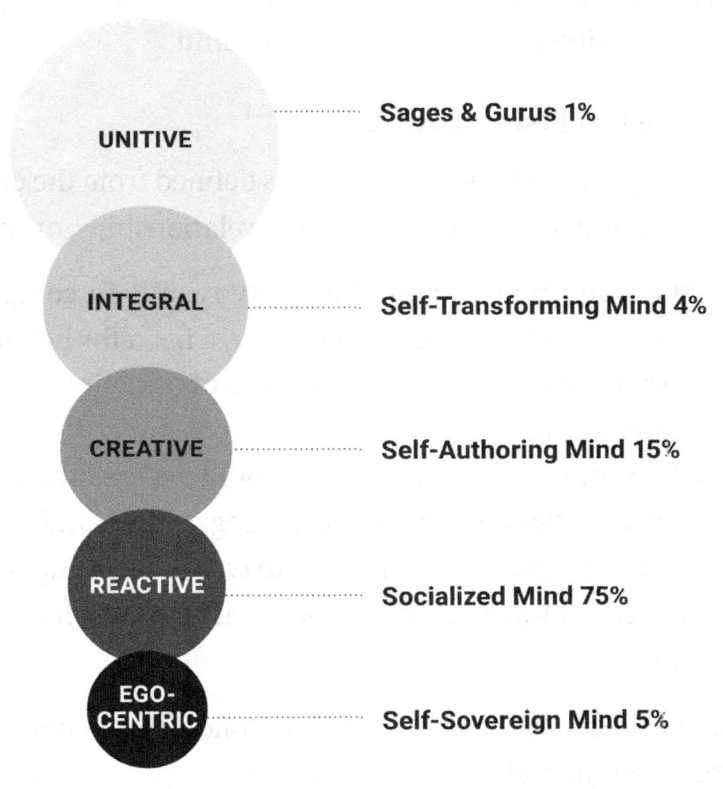

Level	Mind	Percentage
UNITIVE	Sages & Gurus	1%
INTEGRAL	Self-Transforming Mind	4%
CREATIVE	Self-Authoring Mind	15%
REACTIVE	Socialized Mind	75%
EGO-CENTRIC	Self-Sovereign Mind	5%

ANDERSON & ADAMS[7]

Let's examine the model:

Egocentric level

About 5 percent of adults remain stuck at the egocentric level, where their needs are primary. They relate to others to get their needs met. Leaders tend to be autocratic, controlling, "my way or the highway." It's all about them, which is normal in adolescence but destructive in adulthood. If you've ever had an egocentric boss, friend, or partner, you know how egocentric behavior shows up. Growth beyond this phase involves taking others' needs into account.

Reactive level (socialized mind)

Externally validated self-worth. Self is defined from the outside in and identity is derived from ideas, relationships, or brains:

- "I am my relationships" identity results in complying behaviors such as people pleasing, a need for belonging, and not rocking the boat for fear of affecting relationships.
- "I am my achievements and my ideas" results in protective behaviors: arrogance, being critical, and distant.
- "I am my rational brilliance" drives controlling behaviors such as perfectionism, being driven, ambitious, and autocratic.

Reactive leaders are either compliant followers or controlling. Defensive when challenged. Seventy-five percent of adults operate at the reactive level.

Creative level (self-authoring mind)

At this level, we can see our habitual ways of thinking and reacting. Self-worth is internally validated: we are not defined by our achievements, relationships, or brains. As leaders, we are purpose driven, share authority, welcome ideas from all levels, and emphasize self-development.

Other behaviors include collaboration and empathy. Fifteen percent of adults reach this level.

Integral level (self-transforming mind)

People at this level embrace their shadow. There is no defensiveness when they receive feedback because they know they're imperfect. Conflict is welcomed as it expands understanding. People at this level don't feel defined by one identity as they can flex according to the context at hand. They embrace paradox and can lead through complexity. They pursue a purpose that is larger than self, showing up as a servant leader and working for the benefit of the system. Only 4 percent of adults ascend to the integral level.

Unitive levels

Highest stages of awareness. A sense of oneness (the interconnectedness of all beings) births universal compassion. There is no separation between you and me. Therefore, the leadership orientation is global: concerned with finding solutions to improve the greater good for all of humanity. Leadership orientation is about finding solutions on a planetary scale that benefit everyone. One percent of adults—often sages and gurus—reach these levels. (Think Mother Teresa and Nelson Mandela.)

Because 90 percent of adults dwell at either the reactive (socialized mind) or the creative (self-authoring mind), Anderson based his Leadership Circle Profile™ 360 instrument on these two levels. He identified competencies that describe behaviors produced by underlying beliefs and assumptions. The creative competencies include relating, self-awareness, authenticity, systems awareness, and achieving. The reactive tendencies manifest as behaviors such as complying (people pleasing), protecting (such as critical and arrogant), and controlling (e.g., autocratic and perfectionistic). Research shows that the creative competencies are highly correlated with leadership effectiveness and business performance, whereas the reactive tendencies are inversely correlated.

Even though most of us dwell at the socialized/reactive level, there's hope! We can keep developing and reaching higher levels of consciousness throughout adulthood. The more we can shift from the reactive to the creative, the more we can grow our leadership effectiveness. This can trap us into thinking we don't have more work to do. However, if we want to become more and more conscious throughout life, our work is never done. (Sorry!)

Growing to the next stage involves vertical development, which focuses more on *how* you think and act than *what* you know and do. To explain this concept, Anderson and Adams use a smartphone analogy.[8] You can keep adding apps until your phone runs out of gas and you have to upgrade its operating system. Horizontal development is like adding apps so you can do more things (like track calories, use a flashlight, or check social media). Vertical development is like upgrading the operating system, which allows your phone to operate at a higher level. Vertical development can be likened to your internal operating system, or your level of consciousness. It's about how you think and make meaning versus what you know. Your very mind transforms.

Vertical development involves detective work. Your beliefs and the ways you think are like water to a fish. You don't notice because you're always immersed in them. So mindful curiosity is helpful. Why do I think that? Why do I believe that? What do others think and believe? Do I accept that or have a mind of my own? What feels deeply true for me? Is there another way of seeing it? Why does this cause such a reaction in me? What am I trying to protect or control? Am I self-absorbed or do I ponder what others need, including the wider community? These kinds of questions will lead you to ask others about their thoughts and beliefs, which may expand your mindset. (In essence, these are self-coaching questions.) Over time, these kinds of questions—in concert with life experiences, how you observe others behaving, and many other situations—will change your perspective, mindset, and openness to other ways of being. You can change what you question. You can't change what you don't.

> "THE MORE WE QUESTION OUR BELIEFS, IDEAS, THEORIES . . .
> THE BETTER WE BECOME AT NAVIGATING COMPLEXITY, AMBIGUITY
> AND PARADOX—ALL DEFINING CHARACTERISTICS OF MODERN LIFE.
> AS A RESULT, WE BECOME BETTER PARTNERS, PARENTS,
> LEADERS, FRIENDS, YOU NAME IT."[9]

So how do you ascend the ladder?

The first step is to learn about the various levels of consciousness. But because you don't "do" consciousness, it's easy to equate having knowledge with "being" at a certain level, the way I did. If you know how the self-transforming mind operates, you may think it describes you, even though you've only read about the theory. You haven't put it into practice. On top of that, Kegan says we all believe we're in a higher stage than we actually are.[10]

The term "vertical development" makes it sound like you climb a ladder and voilà, you reach the top. But increasing consciousness isn't linear. There isn't a neat, orderly transition from one stage to another. And it's not like you nail all the characteristics and learnings of one level and leave them behind as you access a higher level. You simultaneously operate at different levels. For example, you may mostly operate at the self-authoring level, but not show up there in some aspects of your life. You may *expertly* stickhandle complex issues but not pay attention to the impact of your words and behaviors. So, you're at a higher level of consciousness regarding complexity; a lower level vis-à-vis people skills. This is annoying. I do take some comfort in at least noticing (for the most part) when I'm dipping to a lower level yet again.

Bob Anderson, the brilliant creator of the Leadership Circle Profile, was my teacher when I became certified in this instrument. I took the training thinking it would benefit my coaching clients. I didn't expect it to be transformational—for me. Prior to the course, I participated in the Leadership Circle Profile assessment. I was surprised/not surprised when I saw how much harder I rated myself than others did. But a little proud too. I thought it meant humility. But it meant something else. Bob looked at my 360 and said it was time to let go of constant self-criticism, training, and self-improvement. He observed that my sense of my consciousness level wasn't matching reality. Bob gazed at me with his big compassionate eyes for a while, in his fully present way of holding space. He said I was already radiating and added, "Step into the mystical and BE radiance." It was a jolt of awakening. I hadn't caught up to my own growth, thinking I still had to "do" consciousness. It's time to simply "be" my way into it.

> "LEVELS OF CONSCIOUSNESS ARE ALWAYS MIXED;
> A PERSON MAY OPERATE ON ONE LEVEL IN A GIVEN AREA OF LIFE
> AND ON QUITE ANOTHER LEVEL IN ANOTHER AREA."
>
> –David R. Hawkins, pioneer researcher
> in the field of consciousness

Ideas to help you grow

Self-awareness

Even if you think of yourself as self-aware, growth won't happen unless you're open to the idea that you have much more to learn about yourself. This automatically means that you'll start questioning what you're thinking and feeling, and how you're behaving. Where was I aware? Where did I have a blind spot? This can be discombobulating as you uncover things you hadn't previously pondered. It may even erode how you feel about yourself. It's important to ground yourself with the realization that everyone has work to do and you are no exception.

A safe connection

Even though this book is about self-coaching, consciousness raising isn't something to pursue without support. Who in your life can you trust enough to share uncomfortable things about yourself without worrying about judgment? It's easy to get stuck in your emotions and thoughts without a safe connection.

Transformative learning

Transformative learning is a theory of adult learning developed by sociologist Jack Mezirow.[11] He found that critical reflection and review of new information and experiences can transform your understanding and change how you think, and even your worldview. A catalyst for transformative learning may be a disorienting dilemma that calls a belief you have into question. You may realize that other perspectives are valid that differ from your own and understand that some of your assumptions may be wrong. After critical reflection, you may change your perspective, open your mind, and think differently as a result. This may lead to a desire to listen more to others' views and learn more about the topic, resulting in adopting a new perspective or way of being.

Noticing others

Noticing how others behave can help shift your consciousness. When I was a young VP, I felt protective of the people in my division. I'd quickly reach for my sword if they were attacked. One day a director came into my office, loaded for bear. He was angry, saying that one of my teams hadn't met a big deadline. He said it had compromised his group's ability to deliver a project that had been promised to the front line. I knew my team had been working nights and weekends, so I didn't appreciate his tone or accusations. I was "conscious" enough to keep my cool and promised to get back to him. Then I stomped down the hall to Jean, the director responsible. "You won't believe what Jack just did! He went around you, straight to me, and he's super angry at you guys for missing a big deadline! But I know you didn't miss it!"

Jean calmly said, "Gee, that doesn't sound like Jack at all. He must be having a bad day."

The wind went out of my sails instantly. What?!

Jean continued. "Jack must be getting pressure from his VP. Let me go sort it out."

I went back to my office, bemused. An hour later, Jean said it was all good. Jack was bent because he'd been raked over the coals by his VP who was against the agreement Jean and Jack had hammered out the week before. Jack panicked and went straight to me. I still thought that talking to my peer might be helpful. Jean declined my offer and said she'd come back if necessary.

This one incident blew my mind. From then on, I'd pause before reacting and think, *What would Jean do?* A witty colleague said it was like the bracelets some people wear with the engraving WWJD (What Would Jesus Do?). Jean wasn't a messiah, but she was very wise. My new mantra dramatically shifted my interpretations. I couldn't believe that something so simple could be so effective.

So be on the lookout for others' reactions. What jolts you into another way of understanding? Reflect on how you would behave versus what you witness. It could completely transform how you think and act.

Painful events

A very effective way to elevate your consciousness isn't something you'd invite. What shifted me to new levels often involved painful events: my mother's death from cancer when she was forty-eight; my child's autism diagnosis; depression; divorce; and public failure when I lost the CEO race. I didn't want these situations into my life, but they held major gifts. Each one altered my perspective on multiple fronts. Ego development expert Susanne Cook-Greuter says suffering "often accompanies the move to a new level. The crucible of a loss of loved ones, serious illness, disasters and other [issues] are all potential levers for reorienting and restructuring our understanding of ourselves and the world."[12] My life's meaning and purpose were altered. My awareness expanded, and not just self-awareness but awareness of others' suffering.

The aftermath of these events eventually grew my self-compassion, which greatly expanded my compassion for others. This holds true in many other areas. If you want to be less judgmental, let go of self-judgment. Shedding perfectionism will help you adopt more realistic standards, which will affect what you expect of others. Letting go of comparison lets you appreciate what you have. It also makes you genuinely happy when others succeed. And so on: that which you give yourself overflows to your relationships and the world at large.

Other ideas

The Center for Creative Leadership provides the following ideas regarding vertical development:

- Coaching/mentoring
- Dialogue/difficult conversations/deep listening
- Action-reflection learning
- Stretch assignments/mistakes/failures
- Polarity thinking
- Systems perspective
- Network awareness
- Mindfulness
- Whole-life integration
- Societal-level engagement
- Culture change/strategic evolution

These are just some things to ponder if you wish to continuously grow your consciousness. It is a multidimensional pursuit that will affect every aspect of your life. Anderson and Adams say we need to think about the following as we seek to evolve our consciousness:

- Our meaning-making system: what we use to make sense of the world
- Our decision-making system: how we analyze, decide, and act

- Our values and spiritual beliefs
- Our level of self-awareness and emotional intelligence
- The mental models that we use to understand reality, think, act, and create
- The internal beliefs and assumptions making up our personal identity[13]

Being committed to elevating your consciousness clearly isn't about feeling, saying, and doing the right thing all the time. It is about having the awareness to accurately notice what mindset we're operating from and having the ability to self-correct, aligning what we learn as our perspective shifts to how we "be."

Even if you do attain a higher level of consciousness and think and consistently behave from that place, it's not once and done. You're never free from your shadow—the dragon within. Denying it is a good way to let it run the show. You start feeling superior to others who seem less evolved than you are, which automatically lowers your consciousness level. (Snakes and ladders.) The quest of my younger years—to systematically climb the ladder, reach my highest ideal, and stay there—well, that's not possible. You may be wondrous in one area of life and immature or even selfish in another. You may feel like a higher consciousness rock star one day and ruled by ego the next.

Raising your consciousness will greatly enable your ability to manifest leadership as a way of being. That's not a task for the faint of heart. And I know you can do it.

"The single most vital step on your journey toward enlightenment is this: learn to disidentify from your mind. Every time you create a gap in the stream of mind, the light of your consciousness grows stronger.

One day you may catch yourself smiling at the voice in your head, as you would smile at the antics of a child. This means that you no longer take the content of your mind all that seriously, as your sense of self does not depend on it."

–Eckhart Tolle

KELLIE GARRETT

CHAPTER 2 WORKBOOK

ELECTRONIC VERSIONS OF ALL WORKBOOKS ARE AVAILABLE AT KELLIEGARRETT.CA

1. Looking at the Universal Model of Leadership, where do you think you primarily operate? Keep in mind that no one operates completely consistently at any one of the levels.

....

....

2. Look at the level above your primary way of being. Do you behave in any of the ways described?

....

....

3. Now look at the level below your primary way of being. Do you behave in any of the ways described?

....

....

4. What connection do you see between leadership as a way of being and your level of consciousness?

....

....

5. Kegan says most of us believe we're at a higher stage than we really are. Now review your answers to questions 1–4 again.

6. How would you benefit from raising your level of consciousness? In other words, what's in it for you?

7. How would raising your level of consciousness benefit others?

8. Can you think of a time in your life that altered your perspective and expanded your consciousness?

9. What ideas do you have for your vertical development, i.e., to grow your level of consciousness?

Resources

If you're interested in the free Leadership Circle Profile™ self-assessment, which is mapped to the Universal Model of Leadership, visit https://leadershipcircle.com/free-self-assessment/. You will receive your report via email. Once you receive it, compare your report to how you answered the first three questions.

If you want to go further, the Leadership Circle Profile™ is the best 360 I have come across in my decades as a leader and now executive coach/consultant. You need to find a certified practitioner to order this.

CHAPTER 3: YOUR HIGHER SELF

If leadership as a way of being and elevating your consciousness is appealing, consider connecting with your higher self. This chapter explains how to enlist your higher self as an ally in battling your dragon within and a valuable source of wisdom in self-coaching.

> "EVERY PERSON HAS ACCESS TO AN INNER SOURCE OF TRUTH, NAMED IN VARIOUS WISDOM TRADITIONS AS IDENTITY, TRUE SELF, HEART, SPIRIT OR SOUL. THE INNER TEACHER IS A SOURCE OF GUIDANCE AND STRENGTH THAT HELPS US FIND OUR WAY THROUGH LIFE'S COMPLEXITIES AND CHALLENGES."
>
> –Parker J. Palmer, *A Hidden Wholeness*

My awareness of my higher self started very young. I just didn't know it.

A psychologist once asked me to recall my earliest distressing memory. I was four years old and stumbled into the house in my snowsuit. I was happy and my cheeks were red from the cold. My mother had a fit because I was covered in snow and water was dripping onto the linoleum. She shrieked at me about being inconsiderate. My little self shrank back, daring to look up at her angry green eyes. My inside voice wondered: *Isn't the lino there to get dripped on?* And then I just knew. Something inside me said: *This isn't about the floor.* I wasn't sure who was talking but instantly recognized the message as true. That made it easier to refrain from reacting, which would get me in more trouble. I wondered where that voice came from.

Meanwhile, Mom yelled, "Don't give me that dumb look!" (I'd learned to look neutral during her outbursts. It drove her crazy.) I felt anxious and freed at the same time, knowing Mom's behavior wasn't about me.

The psychologist said my reaction was strange. Children usually internalize adult judgments, feeling shame and thinking *I'm bad.* They choose behavior to curry favor. I'd removed myself from my environment, seeing it from another angle. This consciousness isn't common in small kids. (My grandmother did call me an old soul. I was a weirdly perceptive child, partly from wrangling with Mom.) Although my sister doubted Mom's love, I didn't. I separated her outbursts from who she really was. Although annoyed at living in a house ruled by her moods, I felt compassion for her. My mysterious inner voice began serving as a trusty guide.

I remember watching adults and hearing that voice very clearly. "If she were happy, she wouldn't be like that. You'll be different when you grow up" or "He enjoys life's small things and you'll be like that." I used to wonder: *How much of someone's behavior is choice? Can you learn how to escape the trap of showing up in a way that hurts yourself and others?* The answer I heard from the inner voice was yes. I started reading everything I could about God and philosophy by age eight. Obviously, it was way over my head.

After studying psychosynthesis, I called my inner voice my higher self. This sounds woo-woo but stay with me. It's a powerful source of guidance and is foundational to self-coaching. I haven't always listened and sometimes even lost touch. But when I'm tuned in—wow. I'm suffused with warmth, kinder to myself and others, and better at granting grace when screw-ups happen, whether I'm the culprit or not. I feel connected to humanity, plants, critters, and the planet. My higher self grounds me and affects my way of being.

I've heard from many who have heeded the call of their higher self. Bob Anderson, who created the Universal Model of Leadership covered in the last chapter, said he was working at night as a young man when "unrehearsed and un-reflected, came the words 'I am not becoming who I am.' I spoke them out loud and with such inner authority that it startled me. I knew in that moment I was speaking a truth I could not ignore."[14]

What is this inner compass? Various religions and branches of psychology refer to it as your soul. Major religions call it "the divine within—what Christians call the soul or Christ Consciousness, Buddhists call Buddha Nature, the Hindus Ātman, the Taoists Tao, Sufis the Beloved, Quakers the Inner Light."[15]

Carl Jung said it was your essence: "the sum total of the psyche."[16] Psychologist Roberto Assagioli, who invented psychosynthesis, called it your higher self: "In the centre [sic] of the soul, we discover ourselves as a calm, observing and dynamic presence . . . permanently present in the background."[17] Psychotherapist Dr. Richard Schwartz says the Self is the real you: intrinsically good and wise.

In addition to your higher self, Jung and Assagioli felt you have other identities, which Schwartz calls parts. You glimpse these when you say, "a part of me that wants to do this, but another doesn't." All are inherently good. Some conflict with each other (e.g., an adventurous part and one that's cautious). When you're healthy, your Self can be seen as a leader who treats all parts equitably. When your Self meets each "part" of you with compassion and non-judgment, you can heal parts that aren't serving you. You can see how this might be useful in self-coaching.

Like the parts idea, Jung said sub-personalities cause you to show up one way with parents, another way with friends, and still another with a partner. Even within those relationships, you have various ways of being (e.g., "I'm the life of the party." Or "I'm a serious intellectual.") Jung felt you need to understand and embrace these sub-personalities but not pin your identity to any of them. This requires self-acceptance and self-love. (Why are these so hard?)

What's funny is that when you completely accept and even love everything (yes, everything) about yourself, including what you don't like, self-judgment dissipates. For example, I hated my strong presence. It reminded me of my mother, who dominated discussions and picked fights. Learning to accept my own presence meant I had to stop equating it with Mom's. Mine is unique to me. Trying to suppress it didn't work. As Jung said, "What you resist, persists and grows in size."

Ignoring my big personality was preventing me from improving my impact. You can't manage what you don't acknowledge. When I shifted focus to how others experience me, I was motivated to change. I scaled myself back, including how much I talk. My inquisitive nature can be invasive (my husband calls me Journalist Garrett), so I stopped asking so many piercing questions. (Okay, it's a work in progress.)

When I stopped denying that I was a force of nature, I could manage how I showed up. I learned when and how to unleash my powerful presence. I'm finally comfortable with it. My higher self already was. It's simply who I am at my core. There's nothing to like or dislike. It simply is. This was not an easy or quick journey. It took a lot of work with coaches, therapists, and dialogue with my higher self.

Unbelievably freeing

When you decide to like yourself (including your shadow side), you'll realize what I did. Your higher self already knows everything about you is good. This is unbelievably freeing. You'll be curious rather than defensive when you're criticized. When your actions or words don't land well, you'll apologize. Your identity won't be tied to mistakes or criticism. You'll be grounded in self-acceptance and even self-love. You'll have a deep knowing: your higher self is the real you, it's unchanging and impervious to what others think. (That doesn't get you off the hook from managing your impact. Relationships matter.)

When you quit judging yourself so much, you'll be much better at non-judgment about others and, well, everything. You won't feel attacked because you can view whatever happens without judgment, through a lens of warmth and compassion—for yourself and others. Dueling with your dragon(s) within is easier when you tune into your higher self. When you're connected, it won't be as scary to face hard things, including your dragons.

When you initially think about your higher self, you may feel it's separate from you. It's not. Yet your dragons feel like they are you. They're not. You need to understand that your higher self is at the core of you and your dragons are voices that just feel like you but aren't. This will lessen the power of your dragons. You can enlist your higher self as an ally in battling—and even accepting—your dragons within.

More about your higher self

Your higher self is fully integrated. It's at your center, where you are the most you. Your higher self knows your gifts, your flaws, your mistakes, your cares. It's all-accepting. It *loves* you. (Now allow yourself to really feel that. Are you squirming?) There's nothing to avoid because your higher self already knows you, IS you. Your only job is to distinguish your higher self from your sub-personalities and not overidentify with any of them. You need everything about you to be united. You'll drop so much self-absorption and shift to "we." And then a virtuous spiral happens: the more you care about how others are doing, the more you'll receive it in turn. There's less and less separation between you and others. That will help you to ascend the consciousness ladder. Unfortunately, no matter what level you reach, you'll still be human. That means ample opportunities to screw up, love yourself anyway, get up, clean up, and start again. So don't fall into the trap of equating your higher self with perfection. I've been there, as I'll cover in the next chapter.

> "TODAY YOU ARE YOU, THAT IS TRUER THAN TRUE.
> THERE IS NO ONE ALIVE WHO IS YOUER THAN YOU."
> –Dr. Seuss

When you read the chapter about the DRAGONS self-coaching model, you'll see that the "S" is about aligning your words and actions with your higher self. This requires tuning into your higher self. How do you know you're "tuned in"? You'll just know. That's not a very satisfying answer, so here are some examples:

Your higher self may speak to you in the way of a feeling, a thought, certainty, intuition, or a variety of other ways:

- Your Spidey sense tingles.
- You have a premonition.
- You feel deep contentment or inner peace (it may be fleeting).
- You say something and immediately regret it. You may think, *I'm better than that.*
- You hear words: "That's not good for you."
- You hear "Atta girl!"

- Walking in nature, witnessing how the mist floats amid the trees, you feel a sense of awe.
- You feel strong emotion. You may not know why. That's okay, just allow yourself to feel what you feel. A message may come later.
- You may be washing the dishes and feel connected to the squirrel outside your window.
- You may be in flow—writing, painting, gardening. You feel at one with yourself and the universe.
- You find yourself deeply listening to the person in front of you and savoring the connection.

You will know.

If you don't know, try the practice of writing to your higher self (covered later in this chapter) with a twist: pretend you're connected and see what emerges. And if that doesn't appeal, think of your best self. What are you like when you're at your best? Tap into that knowing.

There are dragons within and also gold

Whether you can access the wisdom of your higher self or not, it's always there. Centuries ago, a giant Buddha in Thailand was covered with clay to protect it from warring tribes. Hundreds of years later, a monk noticed a yellow tint between some cracks in the clay. He picked at them and was astonished. He and his fellow monks chipped at the clay. The Buddha was made of solid gold.

Buddhist and meditation guru Tara Brach uses this as a metaphor for our higher self: "The gold of our true nature can never be tarnished. No matter how it might get covered over or disguised by feelings of anger, deficiency, or fear, our awareness remains radiant and pure. In the moments of remembering and trusting this basic goodness of our Being, the grip of 'something's wrong' dissolves and we open to happiness, peace, and freedom."[18]

The key? Find out what works best for you. Following practices to access your higher self cues your mind, body, heart, and soul to tune in. This will help you tap into a force larger than you—the divine, God, spirit, whatever resonates with you. Maybe you'll go as far as the mystic Silfath Pinto. She has two tattoos to remind her to stay connected to her higher self and realize it's always with her: *I'm right here* and *Stay with me.*

Practices to Access Your Higher Self

There are many ways to access your higher self. You'll need more than your beautiful mind to do so. Use other ways of knowing, including your body and emotions. I've provided several here for you to consider as well as resources for your consideration. You may already have a practice or two that works for you.

Believe the answers are within you

Scott L. Rogers, author and director of the University of Miami's Mindfulness in Law program, says believing is key: "The first step to gaining access to your higher—and one might say, best—self to know that the answers to your questions are within you. If you don't believe this, your higher self will remain elusive. He recommends using an affirmation, such as 'The answers are within me. We are all a part of the whole. We all have access to wisdom and compassion.'"[19]

Meditation

You need to quit racing around if you want to connect with your higher self. Meditation is a way to calm your busy mind.

Sitting meditation can be done in as few as five minutes. Most experts recommend at least twenty minutes.

Silent meditation is . . . silent. You're not listening to anyone guide the process. It's just you, sitting in quiet, usually with your eyes closed. There's a misconception that your mind will clear as you sit. That doesn't happen. Your thoughts continue but you don't get attached to them. You notice them and then return your mind to meditation. An often-used analogy is the sky and clouds. The sky is always blue, whether behind clouds or snowstorms. Your higher self is always there beneath the busy mind.

Guided meditation: Just as it sounds, you're guided through a meditation. Often this includes periods of silence to contemplate a topic that you've just heard about. Jon Kabat-Zinn recommends "connecting with what's most beautiful in yourself."[20] Tara Mohr has free resources on her website to access what she calls your "inner mentor."[21] There are many other resources on the world wide web. You can search by desired meditation length, topic (e.g., anxiety), and a host of other topics.

Active meditation

Active meditation requires a repetitive action that induces a meditative state. It spans walking, knitting, and many other examples. I like to walk outside without listening to a podcast. Just being present in nature soothes me. I like noticing the birds, goofy squirrels, wild hares (we live on the edge of the prairie and I just love all the critters). The air is clean and clear. I find myself breathing deeply. My higher self doesn't feel separate at all on such walks. Afterward, I often journal about what struck me.

Mindfulness practice

Mindfulness is about being present and noticing without judgment. Instead of washing the dishes and letting your thoughts dash about, you notice the dishes, the feel of the water, the act of cleaning, and so on. When your mind inevitably stops being present, you gently corral your thoughts (without judging yourself for not "doing" mindfulness right) and return to noticing the act of washing the dishes. As the famous spiritual teacher Ram Dass said, "Be here now." Mindfulness can be practiced in everything you do. Examples include baking, gardening, woodworking, and art. At work, mindfulness can be practiced during meetings, where you completely focus on what the speaker is saying without formulating your response while they're talking.

Emotions

Practice noticing and naming your emotions. Try unbundling (e.g., if you feel angry, is there an emotion underneath, such as sadness? Do you have go-to emotions? Ones that you find difficult? Do you allow yourself to truly feel whatever you're feeling?) It's useful to understand what your emotions with some granularity (i.e., beyond mad, sad, and glad). The more tuned in you are, the better you can soothe yourself, act on emotions that require action, and regulate your behavior, if necessary.

Tune into your body

Our bodies hold wisdom that many of us aren't used to accessing. When you are feeling an emotion, for example, try and notice if there's an attendant sensation in your body. When I'm stressed, I clench my teeth and purse my lips. The more we connect feelings and reactions in our body, the more we can access valuable input to our thoughts.

My former coach Jodi Woollam created an exercise called Easy Body Recalibration, which includes elements of Jeffery Allen's work. It only takes five to ten minutes. She recommends following this practice daily or a minimum of three times a week. Jodi says it is calming and grounding, and it provides you with a reset. You'll find this in the Appendix.

Journal

There are many ways to approach journaling. In her famous book *The Artist's Way,* Julia Cameron wrote about morning pages. These consist of writing three pages every morning about what's on your mind. It's meant to be a brain dump that declutters what's preoccupying you before your day starts.

Journal with a prompt: This involves zeroing in on a specific topic. In the quest for connection to your higher self, you may want to answer questions like: What do I know about my higher self? What do I wish I could know? What qualities define this part of me? Another approach is to ask yourself: Who am I at my core? What defines me and is unchanging, no matter what happens? Answers to these questions are clues to your essence, your soul, your true nature, or your higher self.

Seek guidance

Some people give their higher self a name and seek guidance. Writer Elizabeth Gilbert asks, "Dear Love: what would you have me know today?" She then engages in stream of consciousness writing. She's used this practice for twenty years and views it as "the single most important relationship in my life, and the foundation of my spiritual work." Gilbert defines Love as Infinite Love / Unconditional Love, not romantic love. She says she hears messages like "I don't need you to be any different than you are . . . No matter how today's drama or dilemma resolves itself, I will be right here with you." Love doesn't need anything from me. She just loves me."[22]

I belong to Gilbert's *Substack* community. Every day, members post their "Letters from Love." They reveal huge tenderness from Love, their higher self, or whomever they've chosen to write. There are squishy endearments like "Dear Little Squirrel" or "Dear sweet one." One of mine was "You know you don't do well in front of a platter of cheese, dear heart."

Thinking about one's higher self as a source of unconditional love is the idea here. You can use a different name from Love. I write "Dear Higher Self" on days I'm trying to connect with my higher self. When I want to tap into spiritual wisdom, I write "Dear Go-od, what would you have me know today?" (I don't adhere to a structured religion and believe God is the distillation of all goodness. So I add an "o" to God and tune into that.)

Another idea is to ponder what's preoccupying you and then ask for guidance from your higher self. For example, when you've lost your mojo, you may ask questions such as:

1. What is robbing me of energy? How am I feeling?
2. Now think of other times where you felt dragged down: What was I doing? What feelings did I have?
3. Think of times when you felt completely interested in a pursuit: What were you doing? Did you lose track of time, entering a flow state?
4. Hold both states (engaged and disengaged) in your mind. Now ask your higher self for guidance with a question: "What would you have me do to feed my soul and regain my energy?" Sit in meditation, take a walk, paint (whatever puts you in a receptive space).
5. If you experience a deep inner knowing, yay! Write it down and determine small steps toward regaining your mojo.
6. If you don't, that's okay. Going about your days with this knowledge about what robs you of joy and what fires you up will eventually result in clarity about the shifts you need to make.

Adopt the perspective of detached observer

Researchers at Stanford discovered that adopting the perspective of a detached observer resulted in less rumination over time. Cambridge researchers found that teaching people to "see the big picture" reduced intrusive thinking (the kind that drains executive functions) and avoid painful memories.[23] What would a detached observer say to you? This is particularly helpful for self-coaching.

Drawing or painting practice

There's a misconception that talent is a prerequisite for expressing ourselves artistically. My mother was a great artist, so I never bothered trying. Last year I started learning how to paint with watercolor, acrylic, and oils. It's absorbing and meditative. I feel tuned into myself.

You may want to try a psychosynthesis practice that dances between asking a question, sitting with the answers, and drawing what arises. This is a form of self-coaching:

"If I could do anything, what would I choose to pursue?"
"What obstacles are standing in the way of what I want to pursue?"
"What is my dominant feeling today and what does it look like?"
"What does my wise inner self love about me?"

Prayer

Commonly used by religious and spiritual traditions, prayer has a meditative effect. Some religions include specific actions to assist prayer, such as praying the rosary, which involves ten specific steps. The repetition of the prayers associated with each step is calming. The mala has a similar process, where a mantra is said over each of the 108 beads.

My wise friend Sharon Bergen says, "My prayer life is based on Psalm 46:10: 'Be still and know that I am God.' Prayer is a time to quiet myself, to be present and IN the presence of something more significant than me. It's a time to surrender, to let go of burdens. I try to stop analyzing, looking for reasons and answers. Being in silence brings awareness, calm, and renewal. Prayer is a refuge: I feel cared for and safe—a time of healing and hopefulness. As an aside, whether it's meditation, mindfulness, or prayer, one isn't better than another. Each are different paths to calm and inner peace. My path at this time in my life is mindful prayer with God."

You don't need to belong to a religious institution to pray. As the German theologian Meister Eckhart said, "If the only prayer you ever say in your entire life is thank you, it will be enough." If nonreligious prayer appeals to you, there are many books and articles on this topic.

Nature

Spending time in nature can connect you to your higher self. Pastimes such as gardening, a daily walking practice, forest bathing, and paddling. My sister, Robin Garrett, is a certified hiking leader and regularly takes groups on long and challenging hikes. (She cheers me on when my Apple watch tells her I've completed a thirty-five-minute walk. Meanwhile, hers tells me she's hiked twenty-seven kilometers!) Hiking clears her mind and gives her time in nature. Plus, she says the endorphins are amazing. (I've never really experienced those thingies. Maybe I need to do something more strenuous . . .)

Create a ritual to ground and calm yourself: lighting a candle, saying a mantra, journaling. Make a coffee and sit in silence.

Visualization

Visualization is just as it sounds: imagining something with visual images. Athletes visualize succeeding at a future competition. They break down everything they'll do to prepare and perform. There are many visualizations—find one that resonates with you.

Consider a visualization with the wisest person you can imagine or already have in your life. I once participated in a guided version of this. We imagined ourselves climbing a mountain to meet with the wisest person we'd ever met. We were asked to observe the terrain around us in detail. This fostered concentration and calmness. When I reached the top, I saw a woman with long white hair and vivid blue robes. She turned around and the elder was me. "What took you so long?" she said. We had a rich conversation. Afterward, I realized the elder was my higher self.

Another way to visualize is to create a vision board. Instead of envisioning where you want to be a year or ten from now, envision your higher self. What is this core of you like? What image would you choose to represent it?

Dis-identification process

The goal of this process is to shed your attachment to various roles and identities: "Our sense of identity is often conditioned by our social roles (parental, professional, gender) or by different thoughts, feelings and sensations."[24]

The process follows a sequence—from body to feelings to thoughts. Say to yourself, "I have a body and I am more than my body; I have feelings and I am more than my feelings; I have thoughts and I am more than my thoughts." This process is meant to ground you in awareness of your higher self as an observer and conductor of your various identities. From there, you can ask your higher self for direction.

Self-acceptance practices

Schwartz said self-acceptance is required to access what he calls your Larger Self, which you can't do if you try to "flatten, suppress, deny, or destroy feelings we don't like in ourselves or others."[25] Allowing yourself to feel whatever you feel will provide you with valuable insights. Accepting everything about yourself (feelings are just a start) loosens the grip of internal tormentors such as your dragons. Radical self-acceptance will even result in befriending them. You'll realize they are not you. Who will be realizing this? Your higher self. Think of practices to allow everything to occur without blockage—all your thoughts, feelings, actions. After a while, you'll stop fighting yourself.

Yoga

Yoga is a mind–body practice that tunes you into your inner wisdom. My sister became a certified yoga teacher at fifty-one. (She's admirably fit, unlike her BIG sister. ☺) She says, "I love doing yoga, especially in nature. By stretching my body and connecting with my senses—sights, sounds, smells, and the rhythm of my breath—I feel a profound sense of calm and grounded in the present moment. Anxiety melts away and I often find perspective to cope with challenges."

Gratitude lists

This is a quick exercise. You simply write what you're grateful for. This works best when you're specific. A general journal entry like "I'm grateful for health" doesn't work as well as "I'm grateful to have a body that still allows me to walk every day."

Creating ambiance

We spend a lot of time in our homes and at work (often the same place since COVID). Creating spaces where we feel comfortable and at ease induces calmness, a state that fosters access to your higher self.

In the decades I worked in an office, I always created ambiance. I love growing things, so I had flowering plants to tend and look at, pictures of my kids and sweetheart, and inspiring quotes. I bought myself a purple glass (favorite color) for water. I had a poster of Van Gogh's cypresses. I did this in cubicles and big offices. This is tougher with hoteling (where you don't have your own cube; you just book one for the day), but you can still bring a couple of things that ground you (e.g., a stone with an inspirational saying).

My home contains things I love: orchids, tapestries, and lots of books. I've commandeered our dining room since I dove into art. Supplies sit in groovy boxes and art by my mom and friends Annabelle Murray and Pat Katz graces the walls. I have an altar with a Buddha and stones below my friend Bonnie Chapman's mystical art. I feel happy when I wander around the house or sit in contemplation.

If you haven't already, consider having your spaces reflect what speaks to you and helps you feel wonderful.

> *"DESIGN FOR RELAXATION. WHAT IS ONE CHANGE I CAN MAKE TO MY ENVIRONMENT THAT PROMOTES MENTAL PEACE AND REDUCES STRESS?"*
> –James Clear, author of *Atomic Habits*

CHAPTER 3 WORKBOOK

ELECTRONIC VERSIONS OF ALL WORKBOOKS ARE AVAILABLE AT KELLIEGARRETT.CA

What do you think of the idea of an inner source of wisdom—your higher self?

If you've ever accessed your higher self:
What occurs for you? Do you hear a voice, a sense of calm, a feeling in your body? Write about your experience.

What practices do you use to tune into your higher self?

If you haven't accessed your higher self:
How might it benefit you to do so?

Look at the practices in this chapter and choose one or two that you'll incorporate in your life.

How might you add them to your life?

Resources

Harvard University has a free mindfulness scale that measures detachment (they call it de-centering), self-awareness, and emotional regulation: https://davidvago.bwh.harvard.edu/measures-of-mindfulness/. There are many good books as well as resources on the web on mindfulness.

You can track your emotions using the Mood Meter app https://moodmeterapp.com.

Visualization: Imagine a conversation with a wise person: https://positivepsychology.com/self-coaching-model/.

PART II

THE DRAGON WITHIN

CHAPTER 4: DUELING WITH DRAGONS – MY STORY

This chapter explores how accessing my higher self helped me deal effectively with my dragons. Hopefully, understanding my experience can help you with your dragon within.

Once upon a time there was a bright, funny, and sensitive child. Her good-natured father took her and her little sister canoeing and skiing, and played guitar and games with them. Her artist mother was brilliant, tempestuous, and suffered from depression. Her parents' marriage was rocky, but nevertheless, she had a starry-eyed view of love. At eighteen, she left home with two ambitions: snag a man and have tons of fun. Work would supply money to fund ambition #2. After earning an English degree, she took off on a sailboat to see the world with her boyfriend and four other guys. Two years later, she married her love and settled down in Toronto. Both ambitions had been achieved.

Her career began in advertising, morphing to corporate communication. In every job, she ended up as an acting manager because her bosses either left or were fired, promoted, or pregnant. Her conscientious spirit and lack of experience led to long hours. Relieved whenever a permanent boss was appointed, she'd happily go back to her old job.

And then breast cancer claimed her forty-eight-year-old mother. Shattered, the young woman felt mortality knocking. She had her first child a year later and was smitten. Max was a sunny baby and she wanted another. They moved halfway across the country to make living on one income affordable. Baby #2 (Connor) was a screamer, and the young woman hurtled back into the workforce four months later.

The same pattern occurred. Her exhausted boss went on stress leave. Being acting director during government budget time was no fun. She fled to a less demanding job. Her manager left and she was appointed acting assistant VP. When urged to apply for the permanent post, she declined. But her VP prevailed. At thirty-five, she stopped acting like a manager and was officially Boss. Two toddlers and a big job messed with the fun ambition. When Connor was diagnosed with autism, sadness and anxiety finished the job. Hedonism was history. She and her husband had a terrible time with the diagnosis and started arguing—a lot. Her husband said she'd turned into a tiger. "Maybe that's who I really am," she growled, with a dreadful knowing. When no amount of talking resolved their differences, she abandoned marital strife. She took a tall, dark, and handsome lover right away. The gossip was rampant and vicious even though there'd been no deceit. Her ex was the one who consoled her.

Her sons were five and six, and she fretted about their well-being and worried about how the divorce was impacting them. Work became solace, a distraction from personal pain. She hated being home at suppertime without the kids, so she'd stay at work. And when you're talented, work your ass off, and play well with others, career success is virtually guaranteed. At thirty-seven, she was appointed vice president.

A new and unfamiliar ambition took root. She wanted to be a rock star boss. Her people loved having a VP who was real and funny, open about her faults, and good at going to bat for them. They didn't love her micromanagement, crazy high standards, and blunt feedback.

At thirty-eight, she moved in with Mr. Tall, Dark, and Handsome (TDH). Everything she loved about Jay was different from her ex. He was emotional, dramatic, and sensitive—just like she was. He cried watching tragedies on the news. They had wonderful philosophical discussions. The passion was like the movies. He was her soulmate. Mr. TDH hadn't had kids and kept an immaculate house. At forty-nine, he was completely unprepared for living with two little boys (both with ADHD and one with autism), a wife like a tornado, and two shedding cats. He had a temper, and she did too. Where was happy ever after? She kept it together at work but couldn't stop crying—in the car, in the garden, on walks. Already beating herself up about leaving her first marriage, she felt she deserved to be unhappy. Diagnosed with postpartum depression when Connor was six, she pursued therapy and medication. The darkness started lifting. She and her now-husband went to marriage counseling, which finally taught them how to productively disagree. Life calmed down and love won.

Meanwhile at work, she and her colleagues were assigned executive coaches. She received 360 results with new themes. Powerful. Intimidating. Critical. Ugh. Shocked, she couldn't understand these perceptions.

"I just don't see the intimidating and powerful part," she wailed to her executive coach. "I want to cut that out of me!"

"Good luck with that," he said wryly. "It's part of your DNA. You can't manage what you don't acknowledge."

That woman was me. That statement messed with everything I knew about myself. It converged with what I was learning in my personal life. It was the start of a very long journey to accept myself exactly as I am—in my career and everywhere else. Some parts of me are so different from who I want to be that I've fought them as if they were real dragons. My coach's comments hit me right between the eyes.

It's part of your DNA.

Mom had had a powerful presence; I didn't want to be anything like her. Controversial and critical, qualities that had shown up in my 360. I wanted to be like my father. Diplomatic, friendly, kind. Trying *not* to be like someone obscures who we really are. So does copying another person. I'd come face-to-face with a giant blind spot. What else didn't I get? I felt doomed: I *was* just like my mother. I was also pissed off. All that work on higher consciousness and trying to emulate my dad hadn't worked. I felt lost.

I asked my coach what I should do. He used a fabulous analogy. "You think that having this powerful presence is bad," he said. "It's not bad; it just is. A Ferrari's still a Ferrari when the engine's off. It's a Ferrari when it's idling and driving the speed limit in a sleepy town. You can let 'er rip on the Autobahn. But you always know what it really is. You need to constantly work the throttle—holding this high-performance car back and letting it zip, depending on where you are. Until you completely accept your presence, you won't be able to manage it."

I got it. I could let my big self all the way out on stage while delivering a speech. Elsewhere, not so much.

I say I got it, but it was a bumpy ride. With the 360 in mind, I started analyzing how I showed up in meetings. Although obvious to others, I talked—a LOT. I wanted to know everyone's thoughts, but I wasn't leaving space for them. If I perceived feedback as critical, I'd get aggressive. Sometimes my frustration led to tears. (Mortifying!) But I didn't understand: a quiet Kellie still had quite the presence. I didn't see that positional power compounded my strong way of being. But just because something doesn't make sense doesn't mean it's not true. I yanked between all or nothing. When I was completely myself, I often impacted people negatively. I silenced myself and was miserable. I hadn't grasped the notion of a throttle.

It was dawning on me that the hardest person I was ever going to lead was me.

My strengths had prevented me from seeing my flaws. Employee engagement in my division was consistently higher than the rest of the company's. We exceeded our goals every year. I enjoyed many good relationships with peers and colleagues. I met with direct reports regularly and helped them succeed. This led to arrogance: I thought I was a superb leader.

Once I opened my mind to the 360 feedback, Pandora's box also opened. I uncovered many limiting behaviors. I wanted to help every employee realize their potential and thought that constructive feedback would help them. My directness veered toward bluntness, which demoralized rather than motivated. I wasn't hearing about it because I was the boss, after all. I was protective of my teams and not open to criticism from peers. Worst of all, my preoccupation with higher consciousness and altruism was turning me into a very harsh judge. I wrote off anyone who treated my group unfairly, lacked integrity, or played political games. I talked behind their backs. My judgment of their bad behavior gave me license to misbehave. But my own behavior was a blind spot. I had terribly high standards. I was impatient. My optimism regarding how much we could accomplish overburdened my teams. Sometimes, I overshared personal problems, such as Connor's autism journey. I thought I was just being open. But it led one of my directors to caution her team about approaching me, as in "Kellie's not having a good day."

Gradually, I smoothly pulled the throttle back instead of ricocheting between being overbearing or silent. I did the same at home. I realized that many of our marital arguments were about me—what I wasn't receiving or how much I hurt. I didn't want to be self-absorbed. I listened to Jay more. I made sure we talked about his needs. At work, I stopped criticizing people, even in my head. I set about rebuilding trust where it had been broken, discovering I'd often been a contributing culprit. It was humbling and messy and discouraging.

Just as I was climbing the consciousness ladder, my boss threw me a curveball and told me I should run for CEO. I told him he was nuts because I didn't have a financial background. He said he knew I could do it and he'd send me to Harvard Business School's elite Advanced Management program for two months. I said yes. Off I went, one of 15 women in a class of 154 from 39 countries. I held my own in the business strategy, marketing, and leadership discussions. I realized that I wasn't just a Prairie peanut and I had intelligence that rivaled my classmates. Back at home, I made it through the three CEO interviews and found out from a Board member that I'd lost. He told me to hold my head up high as I'd given the winner a run for his money. But I felt stupid for even trying. It was a very public defeat. I told my new boss to pay me to go away. He wouldn't, saying I was good at everything he wasn't and vice versa. (This was true.) I was prickly but stayed. It was beyond humbling. I wrote the news release applauding his appointment. I put together his first leadership conference. Every time I went into his office, the ABBA song "The Winner Takes It All" reverberated in my head. But I ended up working really well with him for six years. This experience pole vaulted my progress on the consciousness ladder. (Thank you, Greg Stewart.) Sometimes, a traumatic event reaps positive dividends.

Many executive coaches boosted my leadership, making me a better human. Therapy complemented coaching, where I unpacked limiting and damaging beliefs. I learned to notice and name my emotions. I allowed myself to feel them instead of stuffing them down.

I noticed that some of my great strengths when overplayed had become terrible flaws:

terrific at bulletproofing strategy	terribly critical of myself and others
clear and articulate	direct to the point of bluntness
great presence and charisma	intimidating, taking up too much room
extroverted	dominating discussions
high integrity	self-righteous and judgmental
open and expressive	demanding that others be the same
speedy	impatient, not present, not listening
sensitive and attuned to others	overly sensitive and emotional
high-quality work	ridiculously high standards
high energy	workaholism and unreasonable expectations
warm	uncomfortable with very formal, reserved people
good sense of humor	compulsively funny, sometimes attention seeking

You get the picture. Overdoing anything has a negative impact. It takes fortitude to notice and manage our patterns and interrupt habitual ways of behaving. I discovered that behind most of my issues were inner dragons—creatures that drove destructive narratives and behaviors.

Two dragons dwelled at opposite poles: Gusto and Never Enough. Gusto shows up innocently enough as a positive zest for life and all it has to offer: life purpose, relationships, adventures, learning, meaningful work, groovy clothes, and a fabulous garden. You name it, I want it. More, more, more. Both my sister and father often cautioned that I wanted too much. They're right. I do. Gusto is about constant stimulation and voracious appetites. When overdone, Gusto can hijack me into a restless state that isn't positive.

Never Enough Dragon is about scarcity: affection and attention. When this dragon is running the show, nothing is . . . ever enough.

Deconstructing Never Enough Dragon

First, affection. My mother withheld it, needing others to express warmth first. I grew up believing people needed affection, and that everyone, no matter how prickly, was lovable underneath. (Mom said I was deluded and naive.) I find many people interesting and can't bear for anyone to feel excluded. This conviction and my natural warmth have attracted many friends. Never Enough has shown up positively with most of my buddies. I tend to shower affection rather than seek it myself. But Never Enough showed up negatively when a close friend pulled away and found a new bestie. I became needy, which isn't like me at all (except with husbands). This just drove a further wedge. I'm rarely rejected, and I was shocked at how much it hurt. No wonder, apparently our brains register social rejection similarly to physical pain. What's funny is, I don't care what most people think. It's the critical few with whom I feel a cosmic connection that drives insecure behavior. In other words, wanting to give and receive affection isn't bad. It's what I do with that drive that makes it positive or not.

Wanting love and affection from both life partners has often led to excessive rumination: *Why is he being so quiet? Is it because of something I said? Is he bored? Is something bugging him? Why doesn't he need me as much as I need him?* Jay used to get irritated by this. We resolved it when I told him that I'm like our cats. No matter how much you pet them, they purr every time and come back for more. You don't think, *Geez, these cats are needy.* You think, *Aren't they adorable—they just love attention.* So now I just tug on Jay's sleeve, and he smiles and hugs me.

Here's how Never Enough Attention Dragon showed up at work: I sought regular affirmation from my boss and peers that I was doing a great job. I was hypervigilant if anything seemed awry. A warm person myself, I was thrown by cold, formal people. I'd get on the same hamster wheel of doubt that occurred at home: *Why did my boss cancel our last meeting? How come I haven't heard back from so and so? They're always out to get me. I don't think he likes me; he never cracks a smile.*

Not productive at all. I got much better at not requiring so much attention, but it was a long road.

Another way this dragon manifested itself was humor. I'm naturally funny but got compulsive at times. I loved the laughter I could get. But this sometimes distracted meetings and wasn't productive. At social gatherings, I often hogged the spotlight. The happier in my skin I got, the less I needed to do this.

Perfecto Dragon

My quest to be a great boss gave birth to perfectionism. I named this dragon Perfecto. As I confessed earlier, I wasn't driven at all as a young woman. But work soothed my soul during difficult life periods, and I rocketed up the ranks. Being an executive offered influence and power, and the money was intoxicating. But I became a workaholic because everything needed to be perfect. This also fueled credential seeking. I needed to have unimpeachable knowledge. I pursued a graduate degree in leadership. I polished my thesis to death. I earned a Positive Psychology certificate, became certified as an executive coach and then a corporate board director. Then there was a slew of certifications in every assessment imaginable.

When I was criticized about anything, I couldn't handle it. It meant I wasn't perfect. And not to be perfect was to lack worthiness. That is not a fun place to be.

Have I completely conquered my dragons? Absolutely not. It's a lifelong quest. (Very annoying.) I still find myself glued to my office chair because Perfecto is fueling a need to produce ridiculously high-quality work. When I feel misunderstood or neglected, Never Enough starts up: "you're unlovable." Sometimes I eat too much cheese washed down with wine, and Gusto smiles. The difference is that I am super familiar with my dragons and how they drive unproductive thoughts, feelings, and behavior. Although not easy, I recover and get back on track. Seeing what you're facing down isn't as scary as fencing in the dark.

I quit my corporate job at fifty-three. I thought I'd ease into starting my own business. Lo and behold, I had not slayed Perfecto or Never Enough. They'd just been napping. Work started falling out of the sky. Every consulting gig and speech had to be perfect. Within a year, I had far more than I could handle. I'm on year ten. Until last year, I worked as much as I did as an executive. As the Zen saying goes, "Wherever you go, there you are."

Life is easier today. I rarely overreact. Rumination isn't constant. I let relationships go that have run their course. I say yes to coaching that helps people get out of their own way, speaking engagements that make a difference, and boards in sync with my purpose. (Right now, it's the Mental Health Commission of Canada and the International Coaching Federation.) I'm finally slooowly learning boundaries and saying no to work that doesn't inspire me. I now enjoy generous amounts of down time. I cherish evenings with my husband, grown kids, and close friends. We love traveling. I garden my brains out during Saskatchewan's short summers. (If you're going to pursue something with gusto, a garden produces shocking beauty.) I took up art last year, which feeds my soul. Most days are infused with inner peace, which was elusive for much of my life. I never tire of its presence.

The coaching process helped me identify and manage my dragons. This fascinated me. I decided what I wanted to be different, had aha's about habitual behaviors and ineffective thought loops, tried various practices to change, failed and tried again. Ultimately, new behaviors took root and a new way of being emerged. The consciousness growth I'd sought happened, bit by bit. After each coaching engagement, my coaches provided me with ideas to sustain the momentum. In essence, I was equipped to coach myself. Intrigued, I delved into self-coaching, trying out various techniques.

Embracing the light and the dark

When I embarked in earnest on my consciousness journey, my self-criticism intensified. The more I grew curious about my impact, the more I found to fix. I beat myself up about working so much when my kids were small, dominating discussions, and giving up on my first marriage. I also found fault with many other things. It's taken years, but I finally feel compassion for young Kellie. I see the bright side of my exuberance. I love the zest for life that fuels Gusto. Like most people, I'd like some "do-overs," but that's not how life works. As Maya Angelou said, "Do the best you can until you know better. When you know better, do better."

I now appreciate some things I did well. Providing both kids with the warmth and affection I craved as a child. Advocating for my autistic son. Being a lay counselor to parents with a new autism diagnosis. A civilized divorce. Remaining good friends with my ex and co-parenting decently from two households. Helping countless people get out of their own way so they could shine. I was a loving daughter and would do anything for my sister. Spreading kindness around. Loving Jay with a deep connection. I am made of light and darkness. It's refreshing to notice the former more now.

I became fascinated by the coaching process and its positive ripple effects on my life outside of work. After concluding multiple engagements with many gifted coaches, I became an executive coach myself. When coaching clients, I'm struck by how difficult it is to embrace all of ourselves—the light and the dark. Yet that's the best way to truly change. As wise psychologist Carl Rogers said, "The curious paradox is that when I accept myself just as I am, then I can change."

You can't address what you don't accept. My 360 feedback motivated me to address blind spots. Our instinct when we receive feedback that doesn't resonate, whether at work or in our personal lives, is to either get angry and blame others, beat ourselves up, or both. Neither is helpful. I'm grateful I didn't ignore such valuable feedback.

I've also benefited from practices taught to me by coaches and therapists. Cognitive behavioral therapy has you unpack fact from interpretation and replace thought distortions. In a related vein, Brené Brown argues that our brain likes to make sense of things, so when something upsetting happens to us, we make up a story to explain it. She outlines a process (hilariously called the shitty first draft or SFD) to swiftly write down how we're feeling and a rationale for what happened. This usually consists of drama that's scarce on facts and rich with interpretation. She says it's important to fact check our story and replace it with something closer to the truth. Many coaching clients find the SFD helpful to identify patterns. Once you notice go-to stories, you can choose a different response. *Oh, I'm catastrophizing again. I wonder what a less dramatic take might be?*

When I tune into the wise center of myself—what I call my soul / higher self—I'm better at noticing my behaviors and patterns, and self-correcting. I hear a dragon's harsh self-judgment and then... release judgment. I identify what needs adjustment and carry on.

In short, I hired my higher self as my coach. She's into tough love and she's always available. Although I've pursued leadership for three decades, I still have areas to improve. What's great is I can reach my higher self whenever I want. She follows me around because she's at my very core. She's annoyingly right. My inner peace vanishes when I don't listen to her. Gusto, Perfecto, and Never Enough dragons still show up, but they no longer run the show. I enjoy a steadily increasing level of consciousness. I also accept that consciousness isn't static. I may be wondrous in one area and a needy soul in another, all on the very same day. That's okay. I'm human.

The rest of the book outlines how you can hire your higher self as your own coach. This will help you to identify and slay your dragons—or at least tame them. Even if you're lucky enough to have a coach, it's great to have an inside guide to offer self-coaching on demand.

KELLIE GARRETT

CHAPTER 4 WORKBOOK

ELECTRONIC VERSIONS OF ALL WORKBOOKS ARE AVAILABLE AT KELLIEGARRETT.CA

What resonates for you in this chapter?

What is the story of your life? What major events have shaped you?

What did you do well? What would you "do over"?

Can you name your dragons?

Where, when, and why do your dragons emerge?

Is it hard to lead you? How?

CHAPTER 5: BRENÉ BROWN AND THE MOTHER OF ALL DRAGONS: SHAME

The goal of this chapter is to convey that the dragon towering above all others is shame. Understanding this dragon will help you immeasurably—not just for self-coaching, but in connecting and coaching others.

"You've got to take this training," my dear friend Susan Mann urged.

"Nah, I'm good," I said, proud of myself for saying no. "My credential-seeking days are over."

"But Brené Brown teaches everything you believe in. And you even remind me of her!"

"Why, because I'm blonde and funny?"

Susan laughed. "Well, yes. Honestly, you'll learn so much from becoming a Dare to Lead Facilitator. And it will complement your coaching and speaking. One more thing: it'll change your life."

I doubt it.

At the time, Susan was chief learning officer for Brené's company. And when Susan is passionate about something, I listen. Off I went to get certified. When I watched Brené talk about shame, I was skeptical. I couldn't really think of a time when I'd felt shame. It sounded like a hangover from committing one of the seven deadly sins. But shame as something everyone experiences often, except psychopaths? That didn't ring true. Until it did a few months later.

I was in my happy place pruning roses when the realization hit. I sank into the dirt and sobbed. I was completely trapped in shame over the sudden way I'd ended my marriage twenty years earlier. I'd started a new relationship right away. I could have waited a decent interval. Somehow, my ex-husband Don and I remained very good friends. Ultimately, he'd said our divorce wasn't all on me and apologized for refusing marriage counseling. I'd apologized for running away. My now-husband Jay and I hosted Don for dinner regularly for years. But I never stopped beating myself up because I lost my sense of myself as a deeply kind person. Once Don said, "You forgave me; why can't you forgive yourself?" Good question.

The question was answered when I fell apart in the garden. I was perpetually stuck in shame because I'd lost my sense of myself as a good and kind person, the core of my identity. Shattering. I'd just uncovered the mother of all dragons: Shame.

The reason that shame is so powerful is that we completely identify with whatever we did. We think, *I am bad.* In my case, *I am a bad person.* Guilt is thinking, *Uh-oh, I **did** something bad.* We're not defined by it. The distinction is monumental. There is no escape or relief in shame—How do I fix myself if I'm bad? Guilt's separation of deed from self allows us to make amends: apologize and vow not to do it again.

In her fabulous book *The Gifts of Imperfection,* Brené says,

"Shame is the intensely painful feeling or experience of believing that we are flawed and therefore unworthy of love and belonging." If we don't feel good about ourselves, we're not going to *be* ourselves. We're going to try and hide this "fact" that we've told ourselves: we're unlovable.

Shame has been called the universal emotion, a feeling of never being enough: never good enough, rich enough, smart enough, skilled enough, kind enough . . . you get the picture. (Hello, Never Enough Dragon.) Everyone experiences shame except psychopaths, who are incapable of connection. Although shame can result from a major event, it more commonly happens in what I call micro-moments: like that hot flush you feel when someone criticizes you during a presentation. Our instinct is to go into our cave and hide out, get aggressive, or people please. None of them work very well.

Turns out that I'd been trapped by shame for years. I had no self-compassion and therefore, no shame resilience. Yay that I wasn't a psychopath. Boo that I was stuck in shame. I've revisited my divorce hundreds of times. Every single time was soul-destroying. The same movie replays, with the same ending. Fierce judgment: *I* am bad. This shame dragon left all my others in the dust. It led me to discount any kindness I'd ever displayed, any volunteering, anything good about myself. It hissed, "We both know the truth. You're not a good person."

> "SHAME STRIKES AT THE CORE OF OUR BEING BUT HAS NOTHING TO DO WITH WHO WE REALLY ARE."
> –Christopher Germer, self-compassion expert

Since shame makes us feel we're never enough, it's no surprise that this was a BIG dragon. The mother of all my dragons. Or, more satisfyingly, the motherfucker dragon. After all the counseling and coaching I'd already received, I was shocked at its power. I felt dragged down to hell. But this time, I knew what to do. I didn't avoid it. I didn't ruminate. I faced its darkness head on.

There's no hack to get out of shame (unless you figure out how to become a psychopath). Brené says the antidote is empathy—for yourself and others. In her book *Dare to Lead*, she shares the wisdom of self-compassion expert Kristin Neff, who has many practices to grow self-compassion. (I highly recommend *The Mindful Self-Compassion Workbook*, which she coauthored with Christopher Germer. I've given it to countless executive coaching clients.)

It's not like I was a stranger to self-compassion. But I never understood how to turn it inward until I finally got its purpose. Just thinking *I'm gonna show me some love* ain't it. You need to pinpoint what's hurting so you can accurately direct self-compassion at the wound, not just blast it all over. I felt deep compassion for those around me. But when my hyperactive inner dragons were running the show? Not so much.

The center of my vision board for the past several years has remained the same: "I have enough, I do enough, I am enough." I've kept it on the wall as it will be a theme for a long time (maybe forever). Diving into Brené's work on worthiness and shame has been simultaneously encouraging and discouraging. I still equate who I am with what I do. I worked seven days a week a few times last year and felt depleted (also dumb, because I should know better). It's a deep-seated feeling of scarcity. That Brené Brown, she's a smarty-pants. Learning about her work deepened what I'd already figured out, dragon-wise. It also made me a better coach, parent, and partner.

Shame is a major dragon

Every time I have the privilege of delivering the Dare to Lead™ program developed by Brené, I'm reminded again that shame is pervasive and damaging. It can masquerade as an inner critic, an aspect of our dragons. Shame makes us feel we don't deserve love or belonging. Understanding the vulnerability that accompanies shame has helped immensely in my executive coaching practice and in my personal life.

To get the best out of others, our job as leaders, parents, partners, and friends is to avoid shaming them. It's painful enough to receive feedback that isn't positive. Being aware of your own shame triggers and alert to what triggers others is the foundation for constructive relationships. Being proficient at offering empathy to others as well as yourself can help you move through shame when it inevitably occurs.

At the risk of sounding like an over-the-top fan, I can't get over how Brené's work has affected my life. (Susan was right.) The overarching shift is awareness: not only about shame, but about how difficult I find vulnerability. I can talk about major challenges in my life without being truly vulnerable. I can recite my story without tapping into feeling. It is the head telling the story, not the heart, which is nicely armored up. It was shocking to discover how invulnerable I was, even when alone. I felt cracked open. It was oddly freeing. It made me *feel* Brené's work. It takes ongoing courage to be authentically vulnerable, but I'm committed to living there.

Self-compassion and other-focused concern go hand in hand. So if you think that providing yourself with compassion is weak, reframe it and remember you'll be better at empathy toward others if you get better at self-compassion.

> "WE CAN'T PRACTICE COMPASSION WITH OTHER PEOPLE IF WE CAN'T TREAT OURSELVES KINDLY."
> –Brené Brown

So why do I say this phenomenal woman changed my life? After all, I've pursued a slew of leadership certifications, earned a graduate degree in leadership, became an executive coach, taken personal development courses, read self-help books, and seen counselors. I'd already read Brené's books. I thought I had "done the work."

Transforming how I live and work

In a way, what I experienced during the Dare to Lead certification process integrated my learnings from academia, work, coaching, therapy, and life itself. There were several takeaways that have truly transformed how I live and work.

1) Accepting shame (gulp) as an ever-present issue in myself and others

As mentioned earlier, I thought shame only occurred with

monstrous events (e.g., murder, adultery, fraud). I had no idea it could occur in micro-moments. This revolutionized my relationships. Even the stoic are sensitive to criticism. Providing any kind of feedback (if it's a compliment, we don't call it feedback) opens the other person to feeling attacked and potentially shamed. And that's such a painful experience, they can't hear the gold in your comments. This knowledge informs how I coach leaders. If your goal is to ensure others are open to your advice, feedback, or anything else, you need to be mindful of shame. You can't nuke this dragon. The best you can do is recognize when it roars into view and reduce its power with compassion, for another or yourself.

2) Allowing myself to actually feel my emotions and notice how they affect me

My upbringing gave me a great aversion to drama. I learned to stuff emotions down. I was the only woman on an executive team for ten years. Emotion popped up at very inconvenient times: in the boardroom when hijacked by frustration, or if I felt misunderstood. I was mortified when I cried in front of the men. The more I tried to stop, the more the tears flowed. I'd flee the boardroom, coming back to an awkward silence. It didn't happen often, but it always threw me. I didn't understand that suppressing emotion backfires.

I'd thought I was highly emotionally intelligent because I'm attuned to others' moods and regularly dissect my emotions. But it's often been an intellectual exercise. It's one thing to analyze an emotion. It's quite another to feel it. Allowing myself to truly feel is . . . well, vulnerable and uncomfortable.

Brené's emphasis on vulnerability as the foundation for living a wholehearted life and forging authentic connection with others forced me to face squirmy feelings and mostly stop living in my overthinking head.

One coach who was also a psychologist (Dr. Jay Lewis) helped me with this long before I met Brené. He used gardening as an analogy. When a seed starts sprouting, you don't put your hand over it and turn it this way and that. You'd stunt its growth. You water and watch it, but then leave it alone so it can grow into a flower. Jay told me that as soon as I detected any emotion, I grabbed it and started overanalyzing. But it hadn't had a chance to grow. If I felt angry, I'd stuff it down because I viewed it as negative. Yet if I just allowed myself to feel it, I might find out that underneath, I was hurt. He urged me to allow myself to feel whatever I felt. (Sounds obvious, but it wasn't to me.) That way, the emotion can mature into whatever it's meant to become. While I was good at dissecting emotions intellectually, I wasn't into feeling them. It's still an ongoing journey, one that took off after my certification in Dare to Lead.

3) Self-compassion for me and empathy for others

As much as I've prided myself on being a caring person, I've never been good at extending care to myself. During my graduate degree in leadership, my professor Cathy McKenzie asked if I considered myself a harsh self-judge. "Oh yes," I replied, eager to display self-awareness, and shared multiple examples. She asked if we can judge ourselves harshly without harshly judging others. I replied yes and shared multiple ways I didn't judge others. She just looked at me steadily, with a faint smile. (This is a great coaching technique: sitting in silence.) I ran out of gas. Gawd. Maybe she was right. I was judging everyone, starting with me. I certainly didn't make the connection to self-compassion. During my Dare to Lead certification, I learned that growing empathy for others is only possible when we extend ourselves compassion (i.e., turn empathy inward).

4) Slaying the dragon Perfecto—okay, managing it

Perfectionism is the antithesis of self-compassion. I thought perfectionism didn't apply to me because I was messy and chaotic. I equated perfectionism with organizational skills and cleanliness. I was conscientious and delivered quality stuff but thought everyone did. It was late in my career before I realized my standards were unreasonable. Then I started noticing that it applied to almost every area of my life. My garden became a masterpiece of perennials in every hue, without weeds. My relationship with my husband also needed to be perfect. (One day early in our marriage, he wailed, "Can't I ever have a day when I'm slightly off?") Every little thing became a thing. I judged my parenting as never enough. It was exhausting. In *The Gifts of Imperfection,* Brené shares ten guideposts to wholehearted living. On one side, she has a list of things to let go of. The other side has a list of what to cultivate. Guess what? Letting go of perfectionism requires cultivating self-compassion.

> "RESEARCH SHOWS THAT PERFECTIONISM HAMPERS SUCCESS. IN FACT, IT'S OFTEN THE PATH TO DEPRESSION, ANXIETY, ADDICTION AND LIFE PARALYSIS. UNDERSTANDING THE DIFFERENCE BETWEEN HEALTHY STRIVING AND PERFECTIONISM IS CRITICAL TO LAYING DOWN THE SHIELD AND PICKING UP YOUR LIFE."
>
> –Brené Brown

5) Tuning into my body

My coach Jodi Woollam once asked how my body felt. I really tried, but finally said, "I don't." She looked at me in her wise way and didn't respond. (I think each coach's silence taught me more than all the talking.) I only felt in tune with my body when it hurt (ow) or during sex (yay). A couple of years later, Brené's teaching about tuning into your body's signals when you feel shame was a game changer. She calls them "tells," like poker. The body gives us clues before emotions and thoughts take over. I'm still not proficient at tuning into what my body is telling me, but at least I use it as a form of intelligence now, one that I value as much as my head.

At the end of the Dare to Lead program, Brené suggests you rewrite your story. She says, "When we deny our stories, they define us. When we own our stories, we get to write a brave new ending." That's what I've done. I've (mostly) forgiven myself. I now feel some compassion for the young woman I was, unknowingly suffering from postpartum depression and coping with her child's autism diagnosis, thousands of kilometers away from friends and family.

Since I became certified in Brené's Dare to Lead program, I've helped hundreds of people learn about shame, vulnerability, compassion, values, trust, and rising after setbacks. I guess I'm a slow learner because I'm still working on all of these.

I'm not going to rehash what Brené writes about in such a relatable and practical way in *Dare to Lead.* I highly recommend this book as well as my other Brené favorite *The Gifts of Imperfection.* Her website (brenébrown.com) has many wonderful resources, including self-assessments. She might change your life too. ☺

KELLIE GARRETT

CHAPTER 5 WORKBOOK

ELECTRONIC VERSIONS OF ALL WORKBOOKS ARE AVAILABLE AT KELLIEGARRETT.CA

Can you think of ways that shame shows up in your life? What triggers this feeling? How do you deal with it?

....

....

When emotion shows up, do you allow yourself to feel whatever it is without judgment?

....

....

If not, how would it be helpful to lean into the feeling?

....

....

Are you good at self-compassion?

....

....

How might more self-compassion benefit you? How would it benefit others?

....

....

CHAPTER 6: FINDING YOUR DRAGON WITHIN

Finding your dragon(s) is essential to coaching yourself. This chapter will help you begin to do just that.

Now it's time to find your dragon within. Or maybe two or three...

As a reminder, dragons consist of a dark triad: inner critics, limiting beliefs, and protective behaviors that don't serve you. I've already confessed that dragons were behind most of my coaching issues. Never Enough, Gusto, and Perfecto ran the show. I couldn't kill them off, but understanding how they drove negative feelings, thoughts, and behaviors helped me tame them. This resulted in fantastic growth.

Identifying your dragon(s) within is key to self-coaching. You can't battle an opponent you can't see. Here are some ideas to help you find your dragons.

The voices in your head

An exercise I use in leadership programs is called The Voices in My Head. It's one of the best ways to unearth your dragons. Participants write down as many voices as they can think of. They usually use the second person:

You're not good enough.
You're not smart enough.
You're so stupid.

You're a failure.
No one likes you.
What makes you think you can do this?
You don't belong.
You just don't learn.
You've really blown it this time.
You're not professional enough.
You don't have what it takes.
You're not good enough to sit at this table.
You'll make a fool of yourself if you do this.
Only you would make this kind of mistake.

Participants compare notes and realize two things:

1. Voices are *very* nasty.
2. Everyone has them, which is oddly comforting.

In the movie *Violet,* the protagonist constantly hears a grating, harsh male voice in her head. It drips with contempt and runs her life. She finally breaks free when she stops agreeing with its awful judgments and charts her own course. It's drama, so it's exaggerated. But in real life, our beliefs and behaviors are heavily influenced by this negative ticker tape. These inner critics, a.k.a. dragons, are born from messaging we received as youngsters, from past criticism, mistakes, and many other things. So let's dig in.

Limiting beliefs

You have a set of beliefs that forms a sort of internal operating system. Hopefully, you have some very positive beliefs. For example:

- I'm strong
- I'm kind
- I'm wonderful
- I can figure out things when I'm in a jam

Since you're not narcissistic or arrogant, you also have some limiting beliefs.

For instance:
- I'm not smart enough to do this
- I'm selfish
- I can't risk sharing who I really am—I'd be rejected

Productive and limiting beliefs are often rooted in childhood, as well as good and bad experiences throughout life. These are just some sources. I'm sure you can think of additional ones.

Some of my positive beliefs include:
- I'm warm
- I'm funny
- I have a good brain

Some of my negative beliefs (before I tamed my dragons):
- Our family doesn't get to be happy or "normal"
- I'm too much for people
- Nothing's good enough

Reactive behaviors

From the time you were a tot, you developed ways to survive and thrive. You may have learned to:
- People please as a way to stay out of trouble
- Hide what you really want to avoid disappointment

- Fight for what you want
- Use your brains to stand out
- Make sure everything's perfect to avoid criticism

These are just a few examples of the various creative ways we protect our soft inner self.

Life lessons

A life lesson is something that the universe *really* wants you to understand. It hits you on the head repeatedly until you get it, sending multiple ways to learn the same lesson. In my case, it didn't matter where I worked or which husband I had, the lesson was the same: I needed accolades and affection.

A friend or foe

One way to suss out a dragon is by noticing when your inner talk takes on others' views. For example, constant criticism from a soul-destroying boss led me to view myself through her eyes. She said I was too close to my employees, sought too much approval, was too informal, and was not logical enough. Even though I disagreed with three out of four of these, I started beating myself up, using my own voice. In another case, a close friend's biting comments haunted me. She started distancing herself yet wanted to remain friends. I blamed the rift on myself, seeing myself as flawed and unlovable. In these work and personal examples, the dragon within was fueling the self-talk. It was dangerous because it was rooted in fact: my boss and friend had used the language that the dragon then used.

CHAPTER 6 WORKBOOK

ELECTRONIC VERSIONS OF ALL WORKBOOKS ARE AVAILABLE AT KELLIEGARRETT.CA

Writing as quickly as possible (don't overthink), jot down the critical voices in your head:

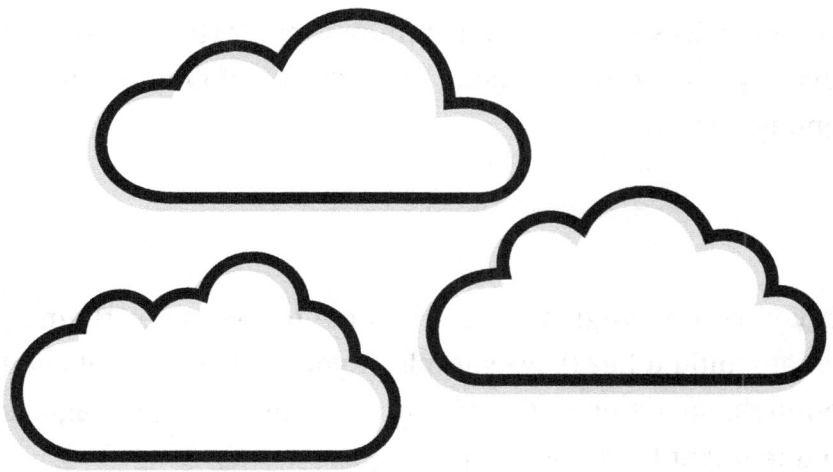

What do you notice about the voices?

Do the voices have anything in common? If yes, what?

Can you think of where they came from?

In what types of situations do you notice them appearing? (For example, when receiving feedback, speaking up in a meeting, having an argument with your partner.)

....

....

Do the voices fall under a common theme? (In my case, it's usually related to not being enough—good enough, smart enough, etc.)

....

....

If you could assign a dragon's name to the major themes, what would it be? (For example, if your voices are not good enough, smart enough, or educated enough, the dragon's name might be Not Enough.)

....

....

Is there a belief that fuels this dragon? (To continue to use Not Enough, the belief might be that you're stupid or you don't belong.)

....

....

Does this belief hold you back? How?

What kind of behaviors do you demonstrate when you're in the dragon's grip? (In my case, the Not Good Enough Dragon drove perfectionism.)

Build on your answers to the Workbook in the last chapter regarding your life story: What are your major dragons? Which ones show up over and over?

How have they served you?

How are they getting in your way?

What would it take for you to think of them as neither bad nor good—just interesting characters who have accompanied you in life and may have something to teach you?

Here's an example of a summary created after walking through the questions above.

Critical Voices	Limiting belief	Behaviors	Dragon's Name	What I need to do to combat this dragon
You're not smart enough	I have to constantly prove myself	Not speaking up; Perfectionism (nothing's ever good enough)	Dumbo	Remember that I was a straight A student. Remind myself that I'm in a senior job. Speak up even though I feel afraid.

How has my dragon served me? (e.g., I've driven myself to produce high-quality work, which got me promoted to VP. I receive top marks on performance reviews.)

Now use the chart below to summarize what you've learned about your dragons:

Critical Voices	Limiting belief	Behaviors	Dragon's Name	What I need to do to combat this dragon

How has each dragon served me?

....

....

....

....

PART III
COMMON COACHING ISSUES

CHAPTER 7: TOP COACHING THEMES

This chapter discusses common coaching issues. The ones I've noticed are congruent with findings from top leadership organizations. One of these likely applies to you. It can serve as input to coaching yourself.

Every coaching client is unique, yet they show up with remarkably consistent issues:

- A need to grow emotional intelligence, including self-awareness and self-management (regulating emotions/reactions)
- Lack of confidence / impostor syndrome, often related to perfectionism
- Trust building and rebuilding
- Giving and receiving feedback
- Political savvy, power, and influence
- Managing presence and impact
- Mental toughness or sensitivity

My experience is similar to a Korn Ferry study[26] of more than two hundred executive coaches, which identified these top four coaching issues:

- Self-awareness
- Interpersonal relationships, including listening skills and empathy
- Influence
- Communication skills

Leadership experts Anderson and Adams identified competencies highly correlated with leadership effectiveness, which include self-awareness, authenticity and relationship skills, concern for the whole system, and achievement orientation.[27]

The Center for Creative Leadership (if you ever get a chance to go there, grab it) identified what they call The Fundamental Four leadership skills[28] required to achieve leadership potential. All of these show up as coaching topics:

Self-Awareness	Communication	Influence	Learning Agility
Knowing your strengths and weaknesses Understanding impact on others Leading yourself Recognizing values, biases, perspectives	Clear, succinct, respectful communication Encouraging discussion Active listening Trust building	Ethical influencing Building networks Inspiring others Building commitment	Continuous learning and inspiring others to learn Knowing when to change course Learning from setbacks Resilience

ADAPTED FROM CENTER FOR CREATIVE LEADERSHIP

Finally, research conducted by Brené Brown revealed that courageous leaders demonstrate four skills: vulnerability, living into values, trust, and rising strong (resilience). Her book *Dare to Lead*[29] offers practical ways to develop each skill, all of which require deep self-awareness.

The themes are compelling. They point to the importance of leadership as a way of being that involves self-awareness, managing your emotions, and interpersonal skills. How you show up in relationships—with yourself and others—is key to transforming how you "be" as a leader at work and elsewhere. Improving in these areas entails vertical development (changing perspective, mindset, beliefs, assumptions, etc.). This requires facing your inner dragons. As Brené says, "Who we are is how we lead."

Here are the topics I've selected to dive into:

- Self-awareness and self-management (emotional intelligence)
- Trust building and rebuilding
- Confidence
- Mental toughness
- Political savvy, power, and ethical influence
- Giving and receiving hard feedback

These topics are covered in separate chapters. Each presents a description of the coaching issue, some causes (including the dragons fueling the issue), and suggested remedies. If one of these subjects resonates, it can serve as input to coaching yourself, using the DRAGONS self-coaching model.

CHAPTER 8: COACHING ISSUE – EMOTIONAL INTELLIGENCE

Emotional intelligence—which includes self-awareness and an ability to regulate your emotions—is key to leadership as a way of being and ascending the ladder of consciousness. If you aren't clear on your emotions and how they're affecting you, you won't be terribly effective at stepping back from habitual reactions, and your mindset and beliefs. Your dragon within greatly affects how you function in these areas. This chapter provides information on emotional intelligence and some associated dragons.

In 1995 the news covered Daniel Goleman's book *Emotional Intelligence: Why It Can Matter More Than IQ.* My then-husband said, "Apparently, you're supposed to show empathy. At work!" When emotional intelligence captured the corporate world's attention, it was revolutionary. Emotions mattering in the workplace? You bet. We prefer working with highly self-aware people who manage their emotions and are good at relationships.

If you choose only one thing to enhance your leadership (remember, it's a way of being, not a title), choose emotional intelligence. You can't show up effectively without understanding how your emotions influence your thinking and behavior. A quest to elevate your consciousness also requires self-awareness, the bedrock of EI. This is an area where your inner dragons may completely run the show.

We experience emotions all the time. But lots of us don't notice how emotions affect our thoughts and behaviors because the process happens so quickly. Most people are aware of the sad, glad, mad trio of emotions but don't go deeper. We may not notice such feelings as boredom and contentment because they aren't flashy. In the business world, norms like "keep emotions out of the discussion" are damaging. Passion is an emotion; others are anxiety and frustration. Emotions exist wherever people are, that is, throughout organizations. Denying their existence just makes them fester and grow.

There are many definitions of EI. What they have in common is self-awareness, self-regulation (managing your emotions), and social awareness / social skill (sensing what others are feeling and responding appropriately). Some experts include other components. For example, psychologist Reuven Bar-On includes adaptability, stress management, and general mood (i.e., optimism and happiness). Goleman includes motivation and empathy.

Self-awareness

This is about understanding your emotions and how they affect you and others. People who are self-aware are realistic about their strengths and weaknesses and seek feedback so they can improve. This skill is vital to vertical development and self-coaching. If you're not self-aware, you can't raise your level of consciousness and trying to coach yourself won't reap dividends.

Researcher Tasha Eurich found most people believe they're self-aware but only 10–15 percent fit the criteria. She distinguishes between internal and external self-awareness:

- Internal self-awareness is about how well we know ourselves, including our *"reactions, thoughts, feelings, behaviors, strengths, and weaknesses, and impact on others."*
- External self-awareness is about *"understanding how other people view us, in terms of those same factors listed above."*[30]

You may be good at knowing how you tick (internal self-awareness) but not great at knowing how others perceive you (external self-awareness). That's how I used to roll.

How to grow self-awareness

Self-awareness (and your ability to coach yourself) requires a clear-eyed view of how you show up. It takes courage to understand your triggers and your default responses because you won't like these aspects of yourself. That's why working on increasing self-regard helps. If you feel good about yourself, your emotional response to setbacks is less dramatic because you believe you're fundamentally okay. You're less likely to beat yourself up if you make a mistake. When you're challenged or receive tough feedback, you're curious rather than offended. If you have a fragile sense of self-regard or you're very sensitive, the opposite happens. You focus on the criticism rather than the learning. Your tender heart can't handle anything but accolades. Unfortunately, this reinforces how you're showing up rather than helping you examine what's serving you or not.

Self-regulation

Being self-aware is only part of the equation. It's one thing to accurately pinpoint how you're feeling. It's another to regulate your emotions, especially when they're strong. This entails choosing how to express what you're feeling in a way that doesn't negatively impact others. Understanding your triggers and go-to responses will allow you to figure out ways you'd like to respond the next time something difficult happens.

An ability to effectively deal with stress helps with self-regulation. If you lack effective coping mechanisms, it's hard to regulate your emotions when triggered. You can address this by working on resilience. Another way to reduce stress and reactions involves changing your mindset about life's competing demands. Apparently, the worst source of stress is mismatched expectations. Expecting to do your work at a measured pace without curveballs sets you up for frazzled feelings. Expecting interruptions and change reduces stress. You may not love it, but you aren't as fazed.

Motivation

Goleman believes that having a passion for your work and the energy to improve yourself are facets of emotional intelligence. Optimism is another characteristic. This serves you well after failure or setbacks as it boosts your resilience.

Empathy

Understanding your emotions and managing how you express them is the "me" part of interacting with others. Being curious about where others are at is the "we" part. This is about sensing others' emotions and then checking that your interpretation is correct (never assume anything). When we are attuned to how others are feeling, we can empathize with them. This is vital to forging positive relationships.

During crazy workdays, many people lose sight of others' needs. Even if you care about colleagues, work's unrelenting pressure makes it easy to push your agenda without regard for their needs. Slowing down enough to have real conversation and express empathy forges true connection. It also enhances the chances of being heard yourself.

Social skill

We're social animals, wired for connection at work and elsewhere. Our ability to create rapport with others allows us to build strong relationships, which enables us to influence and be influenced. If you are a manager, it also boosts your ability to galvanize support and effectively lead teams.

Just like your level of consciousness, emotional intelligence isn't fixed. You can improve it throughout your life.

Emotional literacy

Being highly literate about a topic means you possess extensive knowledge about it. Emotional literacy involves having a large catalogue of emotions to choose from that helps you ascertain how you're feeling. This helps grow self-awareness and your ability to sense how others feel.

Emotions provide us with important clues. For example, anger may indicate that a boundary has been crossed and you need to do something about it. Increasing emotional literacy helps you notice and accurately name what you're feeling. Many of us notice when we're sad, mad, or glad, but it ends there. Knowing that you feel despondent—that is, losing hope or courage—provides you with much more useful information than labeling your emotion as sadness. It's easier to address a specific feeling than one that is more general. Allowing yourself to notice the despondency is the precursor to choosing an action to address it.

Noticing your emotions

Consider noting how you're feeling throughout the day. Or use the Mood Meter app, a tool to track emotions. Whatever method you choose, noticing your emotions and associated thoughts and behaviors is illuminating. Most of us have go-to emotions. A therapist once told me that I did melancholy well. It was my habit to feel this emotion whenever something was difficult. It took a combination of therapy, coaching, and mood tracking to help me shift. I still experience melancholy but it's no longer a dominant emotion.

Understand your emotional triggers and responses

Having a handle on your triggers and habitual responses is incredibly helpful. Shame is often a factor (see Chapter 5).

Think of some common situations that cause an emotional reaction. One of mine was when my teams were criticized by a peer in front of the executive team. I'd flush, feel angry and frustrated, and get aggressive. If I was attacked further, I'd go in my cave and fall silent. The feelings then were OMG, maybe I'm not good enough (shame). Once I realized my trigger, I chose to respond differently. I still felt initial frustration, but I chose to move to curiosity. I'd ask questions instead of going on the defensive.

Observe others

You have a human behavior laboratory at your disposal every day. Conduct a science experiment: observe how your colleagues, family, and friends respond to stress, criticism, someone else's distress, and a host of other issues. It's easy to be objective because you're not them. (Okay, maybe not with family.) Notice their go-to emotions. Are they calm? Animated? Empathetic? Is their behavior productive? Once you've done this, reflect on any themes you notice. Then make a connection to your own emotions and reactions. This may help you shift how you show up.

Interpersonal relationships

With work's constant deadlines and pressure, it's easy to focus on tasks more than relationships. However, whether you're a boss or not, work is done in relationship with others. When your relationships are strong, trust is high and it's much easier to collaborate, share knowledge, give and receive feedback, and influence each other.

Take the time to talk to your colleagues and really get to know them. Practice your social awareness: What are they feeling? Don't assume you know; check in for understanding (e.g., "You seem anxious, is that right?" The person may correct you, saying, "I'm not anxious, I'm frustrated, and this is why.") You can then flex your empathy, responding with a caring comment and inviting more dialogue.

An example: Coaching, emotional intelligence, and consciousness

Let's dig into the case of a fictional coaching client. Allison is a senior VP. Bright and driven, she achieves stellar results year after year. She's in a succession plan, with the potential to be the next chief operating officer and even CEO after that. Fiercely independent, Allison prides herself on figuring things out on her own. People say she's friendly but hard to know. The CEO believes in Allison but has concerns about her ability to balance results with her impact on people. He also worries about her lack of flexibility. Allison thinks this is a mixed message. She says she drives people and that's why her division outperforms all the others; and she's only inflexible when she knows she has the right solution.

We dug into her history. An only child, she was an A student. Nevertheless, her parents often pushed her to ever higher marks, grilling her on anything they thought needed further mastery. Growing up in a suburb, she was bused to school and didn't live near most friends. She was also into gymnastics, a sport that demanded most of her free time. The dominant mood in her household was serious and calm. Both parents had professional jobs and worked many extra hours, modeling discipline and a strong work ethic. Emotions weren't discussed and she was taught to "suck it up" if something upset her. She was a latchkey kid once she hit twelve. After doing her homework, Allison dove into books and read voraciously. All of her time was accounted for.

Meanwhile, her best friend, Jasmine, lived in a chaotic home. Her mother was a musician and slept half the day. Her father worked on oil rigs and wasn't around much. Jasmine was cooking for her three siblings by the time she was seven. Everyone debated everything, using raised voices. And they laughed, a lot. Jasmine cried easily and Allison thought she was a drama queen. While she envied her free-spirited friend's openness, she found it overwhelming. She'd go home exhausted, not knowing what to think about how open everyone was about their struggles and joys. She told herself that her controlled and quiet household was better.

After high school, Allison pursued law and an MBA. Although she graduated with distinction both times, her parents were disappointed she hadn't decided to become a doctor. Allison landed a job at a prestigious consulting firm, where competition was encouraged. She swiftly rose to partner before moving to a corporate job. I asked what influenced her choices. Allison said she didn't like the guts and gore associated with medicine, and the analytical aspect of law interested her. She left law for the corporate world because she didn't like the performative aspect of court.

She describes her leadership style as firm but fair. She doesn't like getting close to employees in case she has to manage their performance. The comments on her 360 were consistent: high marks for results, innovation, and strategy. Areas for development focused on building relationships, collaboration, and empathy. Allison wasn't surprised by the comments.

"I have no interest in getting to know people," she said. "It's a waste of time. We're talking about work here. It's not a social club. The ones who flit around building relationships aren't burning the midnight oil the way I am."

I asked her to consider the COO job. Did she think anything about her leadership style would need to change?

"It'll be more comfortable," she said. "I'll be more removed from employees. It'll be easier to hold VPs accountable. They're used to directness and the need for speed and results."

"Do you think that VPs still have relationship needs?" I asked.

"I know the answer is supposed to be yes but it's honestly not my wheelhouse."

The challenge for a coach is to help the client see where they're operating rather than telling them. So, a series of questions and reflection exercises are designed to increase self-awareness and potentially the client's consciousness.

Since coaching involves choosing a goal to shift to a new desired outcome, it requires change. We started with what's in it for Allison to change. Intellectually, Allison knows that relationships matter. But her successful track record has led her to think that she doesn't need to change. She hasn't grasped the fact that the more senior one becomes, the *more* relationships matter. As an individual contributor, you can control pretty much everything you produce. You're reliant on you. Once you're a manager, your job is to get work done with and through others. People aren't cogs. They're unique, unpredictable, good at some things and not others, and come with personal issues that often aren't evident. A leader needs to harness each person's distinctive motivations, strengths, and challenges to find a way to bring out their best. This means creating a relationship built on solid trust. Only then will each person feel safe enough to ask for help, talk about mistakes, and listen to feedback that will help them grow. So what's in it for Allison to change? She really wants to be COO and possibly CEO. I asked if she thought the CEO and the Board may not appoint her in these roles unless they see more balance between results and relationships. She didn't see this as a showstopper, thinking her incredible track record would speak for itself.

Allison shared her division's employee engagement scores, which were very similar to her organization's overall scores, a respectable 70 percent. Scores were higher for understanding business priorities, decision-making, and sufficient resources to complete the work. Her leadership team gave her low scores for caring about their development and very low scores for the statement "My manager cares about me as a person." Allison said she was happy with the engagement scores overall and shrugged off the caring issues.

Allison completed the EQi 2.0 emotional intelligence assessment. Her scores for impulse control (self-regulation), objectivity, and stress tolerance were high. Emotional self-awareness and expression, interpersonal relationships, and empathy were low. She also completed the Leadership Circle™ 360, which is mapped to the Universal Model of Leadership.[31] Her self-ratings were congruent with other raters, indicating self-awareness (whereas for the EQi 2.0, she was not emotionally self-aware). The scores for results, vision, decisiveness, and systems thinking were off the charts. Ditto for having the courage to speak up, integrity, and composure. But most of the relationship domains were in the bottom third percentile: collaboration, caring connection, and interpersonal relationships. In terms of protective tendencies, the assessment revealed that perfectionism, control, and distancing were issues.

I had her look at the Universal Model of Leadership (see diagram on page 33) and asked if she thought she was operating more at the level of self-authoring or socialized mind. She thought it was a mix: mostly at the socialized level, with some egocentric behavior thrown in. At times, she's at the self-authoring level (e.g., when it comes to systems thinking and innovation).

In keeping with Allison's drive for excellence, it bugged her that she had some low emotional intelligence scores and was operating at a lower level of consciousness than the most effective leaders. This was the first hook to entice her to consider changing how she handled relationships.

I asked Allison if she could think of a leader who was proficient at both relationships and achieving results. She said the CFO and CHRO fit that description. I asked her to observe how they operated in the boardroom and at other meetings. At our next session, she reported that both colleagues wasted too much time worrying about the impact of senior decisions on employee engagement.

"They kept talking about how stressed everyone is because of COVID. I don't go there with my employees. If you ask them how they're doing too much, they usually overshare. And then I don't know what to do with that. And I can't stand emotional drama."

Aha! I asked if she thought there was a connection between this and her experience with her friend Jasmine. Allison said she loved her friend but didn't want to be like her. It felt too vulnerable. Then she said she kept her partner at arm's length. She's skittish about taking the next step in their relationship because her partner wants more emotional closeness. We had the second hook. She was protecting herself from feeling because that wasn't rewarded in her family. She'd become practiced at compartmentalizing and stuffing down emotion. But underneath, she was quite sensitive. Listening to others share anything remotely emotional triggered empathy, which she viewed as weak and found overwhelming. She'd decided she wouldn't go there.

Allison felt motivated to change for three reasons:

- her desire to raise her level of consciousness by moving from the socialized/reactive level to the self-authoring/creative level;
- dawning understanding that emotions matter in the workplace; and
- realizing her impact on others mattered as much as the impact on herself.

We worked through identifying her biggest dragon, which she named "Impenetrable Fortress." During the coaching sessions, Allison realized that she did long for closer connections, both personally and professionally. She realized that she didn't want to live behind the dragon.

I worked with Allison for two years and witnessed remarkable growth. It wasn't linear but it was steady. By the end of her coaching program, she'd grown her emotional literacy and allowed herself to feel more. She'd let her guard down, asking colleagues and direct reports how they were doing and empathizing (with boundaries). She began judiciously sharing things about herself. She was appointed to COO. But she told me the best win was her decision to open up to her now fiancé.

Allison's story is an example of how you can transform. Her success and desire to protect herself from vulnerability and feeling too much was straitjacketing her. To move to a new level of emotional self-awareness, social awareness, interpersonal relationships, and consciousness, she became curious about her mindset and behaviors, and made connections between her past, her work, and her personal life.

Even if you possess strong emotional intelligence, you can always grow in this area. This will benefit your quest to ascend the consciousness ladder and enhance your ability to demonstrate leadership as a way of being.

CHAPTER 8 WORKBOOK

ELECTRONIC VERSIONS OF ALL WORKBOOKS ARE AVAILABLE AT KELLIEGARRETT.CA

Think about which facets of emotional intelligence you're good at:

- Self-regard
- Emotional self-awareness
- Self-regulation
- Expressing emotions constructively
- Interpersonal relationships / empathy

Now think about which area of emotional intelligence you'd like to improve:

....

....

How would growing your emotional intelligence enhance your ability to demonstrate leadership as your way of being? Your level of consciousness?

....

....

Resources

I use the EQi (Emotional Intelligence Inventory) with coaching clients. To take the assessment, you need to find a coach or consultant certified to administer it. https://www.eitraining-company.com/eq-i/

Atlas of the Heart, Brené Brown: this book catalogues eighty-seven emotions

Managing emotions toolkit: https://www.mindtools.com/amqbd0e/managing-your-emotions-at-work

Tasha Eurich: https://hbr.org/2018/01/what-self-awareness-really-is-and-how-to-cultivate-it

https://www.ccl.org/articles/leading-effectively-articles/4-ways-boost-self-awareness/

Free resilience assessment: https://www.robertsoncooper.com/iresilience/

CHAPTER 9: COACHING ISSUE – TRUST

I offer meaty content in this chapter because trust is one of the biggest issues that plagues coaching clients. You'll examine how you view trust and hopefully feel inspired to expand your capacity for trust. This entails identifying the dragon that is limiting you from building a great network of trust-based relationships.

All names have been changed to protect the innocent . . . and the guilty. ☺

In the middle of an ordinary meeting, I realized 25 percent of the people were dead to me.

- Jack had done an end run a few years ago.
- Jennifer had talked about me behind my back.
- Mac kept going back on his word.
- Angeline had completely ghosted me even though we'd been very close colleagues.
- Oliver had blasted me in front of the CEO.

Every reason for being dead to me was similar. They'd broken my trust. They'd shattered our relationship. They'd proven a lack of integrity. They weren't worth my time or energy. They, they, they. I was struck by how much I used the word "they." I was blaming them. But they deserved that, didn't they? They had done something to me. Two more "theys." Where was I in this picture?

Broken trust had killed my willingness to forgive and move on. My self-righteousness was in full bloom. My crystal-clear memory relived past stings. But something was different. It felt wrong that so many had a black mark against them, a mark assigned by me. This, from someone who championed straight talk and prided herself on owning her part to play when things went south. It dawned on me that my actions were at odds with my beliefs. It was bloody uncomfortable. Judging others had been oddly satisfying.

A few weeks went by. I kept tallying the number of people dead to me. It was looking more like 35 percent. As a senior executive at my company, I wasn't setting a good example. I was preaching collaboration, the need to have hard conversations, and forgiveness. I wasn't walking the talk. I had to find a way to make one-third of the souls around me "undead." I had to figure out how to rebuild trust. I had no idea how to do it.

Shortly after my uncomfortable epiphany, a favorite colleague came racing into my office. "Did you hear what he did this time?" I knew who instantly since we commiserated about him regularly.

"Nothing would surprise me," I said.

"He did an end run after the meeting. Jack's being moved to special project land and Mister-all-about-him Moe has horned into his job. Why can't the CEO see what's so freaking obvious to us?"

"Well Moe got his nickname honestly. Minion of Evil strikes again!"

We dished about Moe for a while. Then I sat alone in my office. I'd enthusiastically done what Jennifer had done to me (talked behind my back). Had I ever tried to get to know Moe? Had I ever given him the benefit of the doubt? No and no. Did I act weird around him? Avoid him? Yes and yes. Uh-oh.

That night I had a fight with my husband and had a flashback. It was the same one I'd had with husband #1. I stopped arguing.

"What?" exclaimed my frustrated husband.

"Nothing," I said.

I didn't want to give him the upper hand and confess I'd had the same argument with my ex. He might blame me for this and every future argument. I went into the other room and was still. I realized the common denominator: me. At work and home, I was quick to feel hurt and judge negative intent. The same dynamic, again and again. I blamed others when I lost trust. It was all "they" and no "me." This wasn't in tune with my real self, never mind my higher self. Not how I wanted to be. Contrite, I went to my husband's man cave.

"I'm sorry," I said.

"Me too," he said. That was easy.

Almost overnight, I started noticing how much "they" populated my thoughts. I protected my tender heart by putting "them" in the "dead to me" bucket. For the first time ever, I wondered how many people distrusted me. I squirmed.

I started listening more than I talked. (Torture for an extrovert.) I began asking those on the dead list their opinions on my team's work. It was hard not to get defensive, but I listened and then thanked them. I sought genuine ways to compliment peers in executive meetings. People started looking at me funny. I wondered how fair I'd been. The more I thawed, the more I noticed "they" weren't all bad. When I treated them as pretty good people, positive exchanges occurred. The more we got along, the easier it was to solicit feedback. I rebuilt trust, one person at a time. It was shocking. How could one person's deliberate work on trust transform so many relationships?

As mentioned earlier, coaching yourself can't occur in a vacuum. You need to understand how you're perceived by a range of people: detractors, neutral folks, and fans. Do these groups have similar perceptions about you? That's worth pondering when coaching yourself.

So how do you get all this data? By forming as many trust-based relationships as possible. Even with Darth Vaders—those folks you think are out to get you. You may find out they have a pure heart underneath the black armor, armor that you likely clad them with.

If I'm so trustworthy, how come you're not?

I open trust keynotes by asking audiences to rate themselves on this statement: "I am a trustworthy person." The anonymous poll reveals 95–100 percent agreement. The remaining few choose "usually." Then I ask them to rate the trustworthiness of work colleagues. The answer is never as high as the self-ratings: usually 60–75 percent. At one company, only 26 percent trusted their colleagues. (Imagine working there!) These polls yield consistent results. Why do we think we're trustworthy? Why is our perception of others' trustworthiness far less than ours? Even if you're hard on yourself, you're apt to think you're more trustworthy than others. Why is that? We judge ourselves by our intentions. We judge others by their impact and frankly don't care about their intentions.

The themes when coaching clients on this topic are consistent: trust is other-focused:

- "I just don't trust him."
- "I've been burned by them."
- "There's something about her I can't put my finger on, but I'd watch out if I were you."
- "He doesn't share my values so I can't work with him."
- "Five years ago, they drove Sam out of the organization."
- "She's always criticizing people when they leave the room."
- "He never meets deadlines."
- "She thinks it's okay to phone work in."
- "He threw me under the bus. He doesn't deserve my trust."

These are similar to the reasons I had when 35 percent of my colleagues were dead to me. Now, there are legitimate causes for distrust and writing others off. But in most cases, the biggest reason has more to do with you than them.

In another poll, I ask audiences to complete this sentence by selecting all that apply:

When someone breaks my trust . . .

1. I usually write them off.
2. I avoid them.
3. I talk negatively about them behind their back.
4. I go and see them to figure out what happened.
5. I'm open to rebuilding trust, but they have to make the first move.
6. I'm curious about my part to play.

Guess which ones receive most votes? Numbers one to three. Then I flip the poll:

When I break someone's trust, I want them to:

1. Write me off
2. Avoid me
3. Talk negatively about me behind my back
4. Come and see me to figure out what happened
5. Be open to rebuilding trust, but expect me to make the first move
6. Be curious about their part to play

The majority select #4 and #6. Interesting. We want others to give us the benefit of the doubt when we break trust but don't reciprocate.

Trust and dragons

So what dragons are related to trust? Perhaps it was a betrayal at work or a tough childhood. You may be sensitive and approach others warily, hoping to avoid hurt. Whatever it is, you'll be a better leader if you identify the dragon that prevents you from building trust-based relationships with the widest swath of people possible.

Breaking down the elements of trust

There are many wonderful trust models out there. I love the one developed by Charles Feltman, author of *The Thin Book of Trust*. (It really is thin—a succinct read.) He says when we trust someone, we feel safe. Our bodies release oxytocin, the bonding hormone. We're open to collaboration and debate and are willing to examine our own actions. When we don't trust, we don't feel safe. Higher levels of adrenaline and cortisol course through our bodies. We go to self-protection mode. We're more likely to defend, blame, and expect the worst. The body and mind are "en garde." Wow. No wonder distrust feels visceral. It is.

Feltman's book sets out four domains of trust, as follows:

- *"Care is the assessment that you have the other person's interests in mind as well as your own when you make decisions and take actions and that your intentions toward them are positive.*
- *"Sincerity is the assessment that you are honest and act with integrity; that you say what you mean and mean what you say; you can be believed and taken seriously.*

- *"Reliability is the assessment that you fulfill the commitments you make, that you keep your promises.*
- *"Competence is the assessment that you have the ability to do what you are doing or propose to do."*[32]

From an individual perspective, this means:

- Care: I think we're in this together.
- Sincerity: I mean what I say, say what I mean, and act accordingly.
- Reliability: You can count on me to deliver what I promised.
- Competence: I know I can do this. I need to learn to do that.

If you think I'm reliable but don't think I care about you, then you don't trust me. Ditto if I'm reliable and competent but don't seem sincere. Feltman says, "People collapse all four, making trust on or off: trust fully or distrust fully. But you don't need to write anyone off as completely untrustworthy just because you don't trust one of their behaviors. Instead, you may assess someone as unreliable (e.g., they often miss deadlines) but still trust that they're competent, sincere with you, and care about your interests."[33]

I became a much better leader by systematically building trust. You can too. Wherever you're starting from, you can grow your capacity for trust. You'll have *way* better relationships with colleagues, your boss, your direct reports, your loved ones, and everyone else. But first, you'll have to take a good, long, hard look in the mirror.

Trust begets trust

Think about a colleague you adore. You have their back and would go to the wall for them. Picture yourself at a meeting where this colleague criticizes you. You either shut down or argue. What happens afterward? Do you both ignore what happened? Hell no. You talk right away or quickly. The conversation isn't guarded. It's heated and direct. You might feel hurt or mad. You'd honestly express your feelings. They might apologize and explain why they were critical (or say they didn't see it as criticism). You'd sort it out and discuss how to handle this kind of situation in the future. Your bond is stronger as a result.

Now, think of someone you mistrust. You don't have their back; they don't have yours. Same scenario. They criticize you in a meeting. You shut down or argue with them. What happens after the meeting? No one seeks the other out. You bad talk each other. Mistrust is justified on both sides. When the grapevine confirms they've dissed you, you feel justified for not trusting them in the first place.

It's a self-fulfilling prophecy. Trust begets trust. Mistrust begets mistrust. To use a twist on Einstein's quote: "There are two ways to live your life. One is as though nothing is a miracle. The other is as though everything is a miracle." There are two ways to handle your life at work:

Camp #1: Actively build trust, check out your part to play when trust is broken, then rebuild trust.

Camp #2: Assume most people aren't trustworthy, think broken trust is about others and not you, write people off after one transgression (factual or hearsay), and think rebuilding trust is impossible.

I was in camp #2 for much of my career. It's miserable. My behavior clashed with my honesty value. (I didn't see it that way at the time.) When someone broke my trust, it gave me license to talk behind their back. That certainly wasn't honest or high on integrity. As I shared earlier, I didn't look in the mirror until I realized how many colleagues were dead to me. If you don't want to be around the walking dead, you need to expand your capacity to trust.

There are exercises at the end of this chapter that compare your interactions with people you trust and mistrust. No matter how different the people in each column, you'll see themes. Why is that?

You are the common denominator in all your interactions.

"They" don't have to do anything different. You do. Noticing my use of the word "they" was a warning sign. Uh-oh. I'm externalizing blame. I'm a victim. I'm being treated unfairly, unkindly, and other fill-in-the-blank adverbs.

Let's say you think people talk behind your back. Do you have evidence or is it just hearsay? Very few of us have proof. Yet we act like we've heard a tape recording. How do you know they said disparaging things about you? What was the motive of the person who shared the criticism with you?

And what do you do when you suspect someone's criticizing you? You start acting funny around them. Avoiding them or over-scrutinizing everything they say, for example.

One way to enhance your trustworthiness quotient is easy: don't criticize anyone who's not in the room. If I thought someone was criticizing my team, I'd criticize them behind their back. I'm not proud of that. The rationale: if they weren't my fan, I'd contribute to reducing their fans. I'd expose them as dirty politickers. But I was playing dirty. So much for Ms. Idealistic, Higher Consciousness Garrett. Ugh.

Weirdly, I wasn't alone. Altruistic people often get right in there when it comes to bad-talking others. They rationalize their behavior like I did, believing that person deserved it. They avoid people they've judged. They contribute to toxic cultures but would be horrified to hear that.

Reina and Reina say "our capacity for trust is our readiness to trust ourselves and others. When we trust ourselves, we see ourselves as reliable and dependable to others. When we trust others, we feel we can rely on their judgment, and we have confidence in them." Our level of trust—in ourselves and others—influences how we see the world. "Our perceptions of the other person's intentions and competence determine trust . . . trust begets trust."[34]

Our capacity for trust drives our narrative. We had a tough or traumatic childhood. A boss was soul-destroying. A colleague's reputation was marred by an unscrupulous peer. We had a difficult divorce. A friend betrayed us. Trust is tough after these experiences. Yet some people trust anyway, grant others grace, check out rumors, and have tough conversations—even if they've had some hard knocks. Great leaders are painfully aware of their own shortcomings—how they've gossiped, outmaneuvered, or let down colleagues, even if it wasn't with malicious intent. If they've done the inner work, they're less likely to judge others and more inclined to consistently build and repair trust.

Expanding your capacity for trust

You can expand your capacity for trust even if you tend to mistrust. (I'm living proof.) What does this look like in practice?

- Granting others grace when they screw up, hurt you, attack your team, or exclude you
- Suspending judgment and checking out what happened
- Going directly to others rather than triangulating (talking about them negatively behind their back)
- Bouncing ideas off colleagues and challenging them because trust is present

When I started examining my relationship with trust, I felt annoyed. Why did I have to be the one to grant grace and make all the effort? Was I a doormat? It felt like the answer was yes. I forged ahead anyway. One example had a big impact. I was frustrated with a colleague's unwillingness to resolve our issues. He'd avoid me so I'd avoid him. I criticized him to others. He wasn't quite dead to me, but he was on his way. I finally went to see him. He said it bugged him when I cc'd our boss whenever we had a problem. (No kidding! I can't believe I didn't see that.) I said the cc was meant to move him to action. He said it did the opposite. I apologized and stopped doing the thing. That small tweak completely changed our relationship. I stopped focusing on how he avoided me, which led me to avoid him and cc the CEO. Instead, we just talked. We figured most things out. We still bugged each other but he got off the almost-dead list. And I stopped the cc'ing.

Expanding your capacity to trust doesn't mean:

- Expecting others to expand their capacity to trust just because you are.
- Blind trust or naivete: sadly, not everyone's trustworthy. You need boundaries to expand your capacity to trust and rebuild trust.
- Letting others off the hook and not holding people accountable. You need a curious mindset to engage the other person in conversation and not just charge in and make it all about your views.
- Loving-kindness toward everyone—some people will still irk you or you won't trust them. You're not a saint. But try not to write them off. You wouldn't want to be written off yourself.

Remember, your capacity for trust drives your interpretations. Setting an intention can remind you that trust is a choice. Mine is: I don't want to create any more people who are dead to me.

A virtuous spiral

Expanding your capacity to trust creates a virtuous spiral: it positively impacts your relationships at work and everywhere else. Instead of finding reasons for distrust, you'll find the opposite. The more you grant others grace, the more you find people deserve it. The more people you find deserving, the more you forge connection. To your surprise, you won't feel burned as much. You can drop your guard. You wake up and realize you're enjoying a wider network of authentic relationships.

When you truly feel I have your back, you soften. You're more open to approaching me to solve a problem. We brainstorm solutions together. People notice we have a good relationship. That spills out and influences others. It's all good. The more you know you have a part to play in most problems, the less you'll feel defensive. You won't criticize anyone much, starting with yourself. You'll ruminate less about who's done you wrong. When others talk about you behind your back, they'll be vouching for how great you are.

"But that's too Pollyanna," you say in protest. I thought that too. Deliberately choosing to focus on what's positive about someone who bugs you? C'mon. Strangely, it's much easier than focusing on the negative. Wondering what's hard in their lives softens you. Empathy creeps in. Deliberately choosing to focus on what's positive about yourself when you make a mistake or you're insensitive? That's way harder than granting someone else grace.

Does this orientation always mend a difficult relationship? No. Will everyone like you if you become truly interested in them? No. Because you're human, you'll never have 100 percent positive relationships (sorry). But you can significantly raise your current percentage. Unless you're really digging the drama of who killed who, you might want to try it for yourself.

How would your stories change if you believed others struggle too? That they're not deliberately out to get you? Examining your relationship with trust will transform the relationships you have with others. That's a bold claim but I have ample proof from my own life and scores of coaching clients. The more you trust yourself, the more you'll trust others.

Remember, when you don't trust someone, cortisol and adrenaline are activated. When you trust, oxytocin is released. So the more you build trust, the better your body and mind will feel. You'll also minimize how often your nasty shame dragon pops up. It's all good.

CHAPTER 9 WORKBOOK

ELECTRONIC VERSIONS OF ALL WORKBOOKS ARE AVAILABLE AT KELLIEGARRETT.CA

Dragons and trust

Many dragons are associated with trust. Here are a couple examples:

- Not Enough Dragon: not smart enough, good enough, likable enough drives protective behavior that weakens a capacity to trust. You keep your distance and others won't know you're not enough.

- Burnt Dragon: You've been rejected many times at work and in your personal life. You've witnessed unfair, destructive behavior. It's easier to adopt a stance of mistrust—others have to earn your trust.

Is a dragon within driving your relationship with trust? Which one is it?

Trustworthiness

How do I want to be? A leader who extends trust easily or one who needs people to earn my trust?

What would inspire me to grow my capacity to trust others?

Are there relationships I've written off? What steps will I take to repair them?

How can I build my trustworthiness with others?

How is my level of consciousness related to my trust issues?

How does my relationship with trust enable or prevent my ability to demonstrate leadership as a way of being?

CHAPTER 10: COACHING ISSUE – CONFIDENCE

Lack of confidence is an issue that afflicts many very successful people. It's a dragon that needs to be met head on. This chapter provides some ideas on how to do that.

>   "HAVING TALENT ISN'T MERELY ABOUT BEING COMPETENT;
>   CONFIDENCE IS ACTUALLY PART OF THAT TALENT.
>   YOU HAVE TO HAVE CONFIDENCE TO BE GOOD AT YOUR JOB."
>
>   –Kay & Shipman, *The Confidence Code*

The prevalence of this coaching issue surprises me. My clients are high-powered senior executives with no obvious reason for lacking confidence. It seems to afflict men as much as women. Lack of confidence is an insidious mind rattler. Funny enough, some lack confidence as an antidote to arrogance because they value humility.

Workshop audiences and clients have taught me that confidence is contextual. Many feel confident about their area of expertise and when they're with close colleagues. Confidence diminishes when they speak in public, participate in discussions on a topic outside their expertise, interact with dominant or senior people, or feel criticized. Lack of confidence prevents them from weighing in during meetings, having hard conversations, and many other things required of leaders. When confidence is an issue, many coaching clients say they'll put themselves out there more when it feels more comfortable. It won't. Get comfortable being uncomfortable or you'll never get around to trying new behaviors.

If you can imagine Bette Midler ever tamping herself down (I can't), listen to this. She says, "I'm confident I'm as intelligent as many people, but not as intelligent as some. So, in the presence of hyper-intelligent people, I'm a shrinking violet because I don't want to look like a fool." In my case, I'm very informal and open. I felt less confident with formal, reserved people. They threw me off because I couldn't read them.

There are many definitions of confidence; I like this one from *Psychology Today:*

> "CONFIDENCE IS A BELIEF IN ONESELF, THE CONVICTION THAT ONE HAS THE ABILITY TO MEET LIFE'S CHALLENGES AND TO SUCCEED—AND THE WILLINGNESS TO ACT ACCORDINGLY. BEING CONFIDENT REQUIRES A REALISTIC SENSE OF ONE'S CAPABILITIES AND FEELING SECURE IN THAT KNOWLEDGE."[35]

An important point here is self-efficacy: even if you don't know how to do something, you believe you can figure it out. This belief reduces stress and increases resilience.

When you're perceived as confident, it signals competence. Whether you actually feel confident doesn't matter. When your lack of confidence shows, people doubt your competence, even if you're very good. Tennis star Venus Williams says, "Confidence can be learned—fake it 'til you make it!" There are conflicting views on this. Some say faking it doesn't work because it's not authentic and the truth will out. But I like Venus's advice. I rarely guess that confidence is an issue until a coaching client reveals it. They find this comforting. This helps to act more confident than they feel.

> *"WHEN PEOPLE ARE CONFIDENT, WHEN THEY THINK THEY'RE GOOD, **REGARDLESS OF HOW GOOD THEY ACTUALLY ARE**, THEY DISPLAY A LOT OF NONVERBAL AND VERBAL BEHAVIOR."*
> (EMPHASIS ADDED)
> –Cameron Anderson, Berkeley Business School, University of California

The impostor syndrome plagues many intelligent, successful people. A recent study found that 72 percent of women experience it at work versus 63 percent of men.[36] If confidence is an issue for you, this statistic should help: you're not alone.

Here are some remedies to increase confidence and perceptions of your confidence.

Focus on your signature strengths

Lack of confidence wears you down. It's in your own best interest to build yourself up. One way is to focus on your strengths. Pick two or three that you know in your bones to be true. Walk into rooms thinking *I am smart, funny, and likable.*

Positive psychologists Martin Seligman and Christopher Peterson created the VIA Inventory of Strengths, designed to uncover character strengths. VIA identified six universal virtues valued in most cultures and traditions: wisdom, courage, humanity, justice, temperance, and transcendence. You can use the free VIA assessment, which is mapped to these virtues, to identify your strengths and leverage them: www.viacharacter.org/pdf/AdultStrengthIcons2020.pdf

Find your dragon

You can use some of the exercises in Chapter 6 to determine the dragon that fuels lack of confidence.

Be specific

Instead of telling yourself, "I'm not confident," replace it with something specific: "I am generally confident about my area of expertise. I lose confidence when asked to comment about something I don't know inside out." This tells you that you do have confidence—it just doesn't span all areas. It's less daunting to work on whatever you've pinpointed as an area to develop than painting yourself as completely lacking in confidence.

Watch how you preface your remarks

Saying things like "I may be wrong, but ... " or "I don't know whether it's worth mentioning ... " tell others to discount your input. They stop listening. Just say what you think, without a caveat.

Pay attention to body language

Slouching, playing with hair, biting your lip, not making eye contact—all of these things (which may have nothing to do with confidence) send a less confident message than standing up straight, not fidgeting, and looking at people straight on. (If you're a neurodiverse individual, that's a different matter.)

Rituals

If you don't feel confident about making presentations, devise a ritual to precede your talk. Serena Williams bounces her ball exactly five times before her first serve. This calms her and puts her in the zone of performance. Rafael Nadal fixes his hair before each serve. This calms his inner critic. I used to have Katy Perry's song "Roar" in my head when walking into difficult meetings. It's special to me because the autism community adopted it. If my autistic son, with his many challenges, can get through his day at a recycling plant, I can get through this. Think of some habit that can settle your nerves and enhance your performance.

Expect dips in confidence

The worst source of stress is mismatched expectations. If we expect to feel confident all the time, we'll be disappointed when we're not. Expecting that we won't always feel confident won't phase us as much when it happens.

Be nice to yourself

When something doesn't go well and your confidence dips, you can jump on the hamster wheel of rumination (coulda, woulda, shoulda). Jump off the damned thing! If you can't, time-box how long you'll wallow. I recommend ten minutes max. Then distract yourself: read a book or take a walk with a podcast. If you really want more rumination time, set ten minutes aside tomorrow.

Think about the worst that can happen – and have a plan

My mother was a champion at this. She'd dream up every possible bad scenario. It calmed her to feel equipped to handle anything could happen. I thought it was just a way to fret. But she was onto something. If you know your confidence dies when you're criticized in a meeting, think about what could happen:

- You'll flush
- You'll get tongue-tied
- You'll feel stupid
- You'll feel like an impostor

Now think of remedies you can use:

- Flushing: drink some water
- Tongue-tied: Ask a question—this takes the room's focus off you and moves it to those who answer. Or ask a colleague to weigh in.
- Feeling stupid: Remember what you've prepared beforehand (e.g., "I am smart and will figure this out.")
- Impostor: Again, use a prepared thought (e.g., "I exceed my goals every year. I'm very good at what I do.")

Expect to screw up sometimes

The worst source of stress is mismatched expectations. If your confidence depends on bulletproof performances, you'll be gutted when, not if, you screw up. If you expect to fail sometimes, you'll still feel awful, but because you expected it, it won't mess with your confidence as much.

Try small things

If you lack confidence, it's tempting to just stay silent in meetings. Try something small, such as:

- Asking a clarification question, which gets you in the conversation

- Agreeing with someone (e.g., "I agree with Jan's point.")
- Building on another person's idea: "I want to come back to the point that Brian made." (validates the other person)
- Using a question: "What about if we tried x?"

Extend yourself compassion

Talk to yourself like you would talk to a friend who lacks confidence:

- "You didn't do as well as you wanted on that talk. But you didn't feel well so you were a hero just to get through it."
- "You don't have to be perfect."
- "Don't let it get you down. This too shall pass."

Remember, everyone lacks confidence sometimes. Former Facebook executive Sheryl Sandberg said, "There are still days when I wake up feeling like a fraud, not sure I should be where I am." So the next time you doubt yourself, just think, *That's okay. I'd feel this even if I were famous!* Know your dragons and have a plan to address them.

> "WE CAN CHOOSE TO EXPAND OUR CONFIDENCE.
> WE GET THERE ONLY IF WE STOP
> TRYING TO BE PERFECT AND START BEING PREPARED TO FAIL."
> –Kay & Shipman, *The Confidence Code*

KELLIE GARRETT

CHAPTER 10 WORKBOOK

ELECTRONIC VERSIONS OF ALL WORKBOOKS ARE AVAILABLE AT KELLIEGARRETT.CA

If confidence is an issue for you, what is the associated dragon? Common ones include:

- Not Smart Enough Dragon
- Overthinker Extraordinaire Dragon (rumination)
- Armored Dragon (protect sensitivity)
- Perfecto (perfectionism)

What ideas do you have to deal with your dragon so that it can stop eroding your confidence?

Try this exercise to replace limiting beliefs or worries that hold you back with productive ones.

Example:

Limiting Worries/Beliefs	Replacement
"What if I don't get the promotion?" "I don't know how to do that." "I'm not good enough to go for it." "I don't have time."	"I want it and will survive if I don't get it." "I'll learn how to do that." "I'm good at what I do. I'm going to go for it anyway." "I'll figure out what's nonessential to find the time."

Your turn:

Limiting Worries/Beliefs	Replacement

Resources

Free confidence quiz: http://theconfidencecode.com/confidence-quiz/

CHAPTER 11: COACHING ISSUE – MENTAL TOUGHNESS

Mental toughness is a personality trait. When it's very high, it helps you successfully deal with adversity, but it also reduces empathy. At the other end of the spectrum, strong mental sensitivity is a gift in terms of empathy but causes undue stress because everything's felt so deeply. This chapter explains the concept and provides ideas to strengthen mental toughness or mental sensitivity, depending on your needs.

"Men are disturbed, not by things, but the view they take of things."
–Epictetus
(Women seemed absent when the Stoics philosophized!)

When I was promoted to vice president at thirty-seven, the boardroom felt competitive and hard to navigate. My sensitive soul took criticism to heart. I'd internalize blame (it's all my fault) and externalize blame (they're unkind, too critical, out to get me). This wasn't fun so I decided to eradicate my sensitivity. (Unrealistic, I know.) That's when I came across the concept of mental toughness. I thought it meant being stoic, toughing things out, and developing an impenetrable shell to prevent hurt. It does have elements of these but there's more to it. Note: Men and women are not more or less mentally tough than the other. Statistically, the difference is negligible.

It turns out mental toughness is at one end of a continuum. At the other end is mental sensitivity. A mentally sensitive person is not weak. (Phew!) A mentally tough person is not uncaring. You may be mentally tough in one area and mentally sensitive in another. I was sensitive in the emotional control domain but mentally tough regarding discipline and commitment. I worked hard to develop mental toughness and if anything, became too tough on emotional control for a while.

The US Athletics team coach Jim Loehr coined the term mental toughness. At the Atlanta Olympic Games, every athlete on his team achieved their personal best, whether they won a medal or not. Mindset and attitude make a difference when athletes compete. One of the fascinating things about elite athletes is their relationship to criticism. They relentlessly analyze how to improve every aspect of their performance. They welcome feedback from their coach. But self-criticism is balanced by self-compassion: "I trained hard and did what I could." Without self-compassion, the endless critiques are taken too much to heart and start diminishing performance. This lesson can be translated to us ordinary physical specimens: welcome feedback from others, analyze what you can do better next time, and feel self-compassion (i.e., "I did my best, I learned xyz, and I'll try something new next time.")

Leading mental toughness researchers Peter Clough and Doug Strycharczyk define mental toughness as a "personality trait that determines how we deal with stressors, pressure, opportunity and challenge, **irrespective of circumstances.**"[37]

The key phrase is in bold: no matter what happens, how a mentally tough person thinks is generally the same. It's not that the mentally tough experience less stress, they just respond to stressors differently from the mentally sensitive.

Mental toughness has a genetic component and is also influenced by what happens to us. You may be mentally tough in some areas and mentally sensitive in others. Both have pluses and minuses. That said, mental toughness makes life easier. Mental toughness has some other interesting benefits:[38]

- Increases performance by 25 percent
- More agility dealing with change, including a can-do attitude
- More well-being
- Deal better with stress and pressure, anxiety, and depression. (Mentally tough individuals get stressed, anxious, and depressed, but they handle it better.)
- Mental toughness spurs ambition and a desire to improve yourself and your situation
- Better sleep (now there's a reason to improve your mental toughness!)
- Seeing opportunity in life.

SELF-COACHING THE DRAGON WITHIN

Mentally Sensitive	Mentally Tough
Feel every setback	More positive
Life is more challenging	Enjoy better well-being
Can achieve great things	Achieve more
More aware of burnout	"I can do it, why can't you?"
More cooperative	Can overcommit: burnout
More effective followers	Doesn't recognize signs of fatigue
Often more creative	Over-confident

Source: AQR International

The well-researched mental toughness model shown below was developed by Clough, a leading academic in applied psychology.

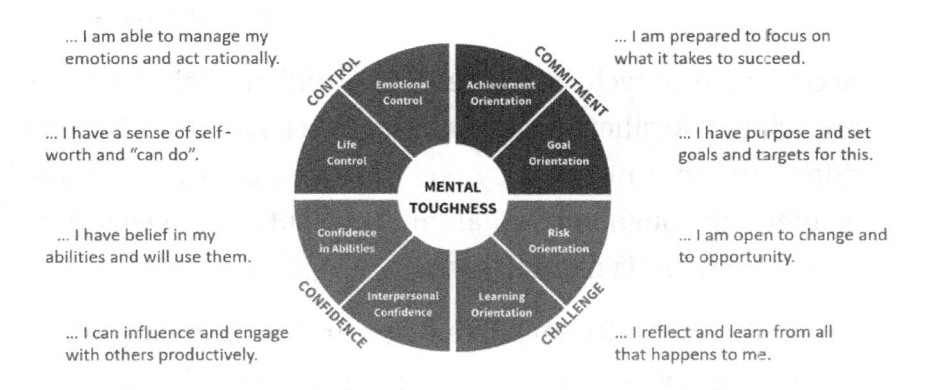

... I am able to manage my emotions and act rationally.

... I have a sense of self-worth and "can do".

... I have belief in my abilities and will use them.

... I can influence and engage with others productively.

... I am prepared to focus on what it takes to succeed.

... I have purpose and set goals and targets for this.

... I am open to change and to opportunity.

... I reflect and learn from all that happens to me.

Each enables me "to be the best that I can be".
Self-awareness is the key – "if I understand myself, I can improve myself."

AQR International

Studies show that "the more mentally tough are statistically likely to be more emotionally intelligent than the more mentally sensitive."[39] (This seemed counterintuitive to me.) The interplay is shown in the table below. Note: awareness refers to self-awareness and other awareness. As with most things, balance is desirable: high mental toughness can lead to lack of empathy, whereas low mental toughness can result in suffering because of high sensitivity.

Low mental toughness/high EI Very aware and affected by it	High mental toughness/high EI Aware but not moved by it
Low mental toughness/low EI Poor awareness of others but easily bruised	High mental toughness/low EI Poor awareness, thick skinned, insensitive

Source: AQR International

According to Strycharczyk, resilience and mental toughness are related. Resilience is the ability to recover quickly from difficulties, not necessarily feel positive about it. Virtually all mentally tough individuals are resilient but not everyone who is resilient is mentally tough.

If you're mentally sensitive, you can increase your effectiveness and lessen stress by increasing mental toughness. If you're mentally tough, you can enhance your impact on others by developing more sensitivity and empathy. Becoming aware of our default reaction is the first step to choosing a different response.

Well-being is related to mental toughness

Think of this scenario: Someone shouts at us. The mentally sensitive feel it is directed at them. Mentally tough folks think the person has trouble controlling themselves, and they don't take it personally. In addition, the mentally tough are more apt to mine the gold in criticism, no matter how it was delivered.

Mental toughness is a fascinating concept. No matter which end of the mental toughness continuum you're at, self-awareness will help enhance your effectiveness: choose where you need to increase or decrease your mental toughness and mental sensitivity to optimize your strengths and mitigate weaknesses. This will be useful in your quest to demonstrate leadership behaviors and grow your level of consciousness.

> "MENTAL TOUGHNESS IS OFTEN PORTRAYED AS DETERMINATION AND PERSISTENCE, BUT IT CAN ALSO BE FLEXIBILITY AND ADAPTABILITY: I CAN BE HAPPY ANYWHERE, I CAN WORK WITH WHAT I HAVE, I CAN HAVE A GOOD DAY WITH ANYONE. YOU ARE TOUGH WHEN YOUR MOOD IS NOT DEPENDENT ON YOUR CIRCUMSTANCES."
>
> –James Clear, author of *Atomic Habits*

KELLIE GARRETT

CHAPTER 11 WORKBOOK

ELECTRONIC VERSIONS OF ALL WORKBOOKS ARE AVAILABLE AT KELLIEGARRETT.CA

Where do you think you fall on the mental toughness continuum? Are you high in mental toughness or mental sensitivity?

Use the model on page 161 to select which dimensions of mental toughness you'd like to work on.

How might your mental toughness or mental sensitivity help or hinder your quest to demonstrate leadership as a way of being?

What dragon might be associated with this topic? See the examples below to spur your thinking:

Dragons associated with mental sensitivity	Dragons associated with mental toughness
Emotional Dragon	Cold Dragon
Not Good Enough Dragon	Achievement Dragon
Thin-Skinned Dragon	Arrogant Dragon
The World Is Out to Get Me Dragon	No Empathy Dragon

Once you've landed on your dragon, write about how it fuels too much mental sensitivity or mental toughness.

What might you try to combat your dragon and grow your mental toughness or mental sensitivity (if you lack empathy)?

Resources

If you're interested in understanding your level of mental toughness, coaches certified by AQR can administer the assessment.

Developing Mental Toughness, Dr. Peter Clough & Doug Strycharczyk.

Grit, Angela Duckworth. Her website has a free grit self-assessment.

Mindset: The New Psychology of Success, Carol Dweck

Dr. Nick Lazaris, www.fearlessforlife.com

Mental Toughness program https://aqrinternational.co.uk/product/mental-toughness-development-online-programme?mc_cid=5ec8eac313&mc_eid=7b0c0c04fb

Learned Optimism, Martin Seligman

Mental Toughness and Emotional Intelligence, Doug Strycharczyk, April 19, 2021, https://aqrinternational.co.uk/mental-toughness-emotional-intelligence

The Mental Toughness Handbook, Damon Zahariades

CHAPTER 12: COACHING ISSUE – POLITICAL SAVVY AND POWER

Political savvy means understanding your organization's networks, where power lies and how influence occurs. Many altruistic clients refuse to "play the game." Changing your relationship with political savvy and power may entail battling dragons.

"Choose any two competent people, and the one who has political savvy, agility in the use of power, and the ability to influence others will go further."
–Kathleen Kelly Reardon[40]

Political savvy is one of the crunchiest topics I encounter with coaching clients. One client said he hates politics. "The ones who are good at it aren't honest," he said.

"So they're dishonest?" I asked. He squirmed.

"Sometimes, yes. It's more like they're completely self-interested."

"Can they be self-interested and also interested in what's good for others?"

"I don't think so."

"Is it all or nothing?"

Like this client, I used to proudly proclaim that I didn't play politics. I'm a straight shooter and couldn't fathom hidden agendas. I'd create problems for myself and my teams by failing to see when we were making another group look bad or failing to socialize a strategy before bringing it to the boardroom.

Despite holding a powerful executive VP position, this client felt excluded from the CEO's inner circle. At the same time, he viewed the colleagues who were included as people who sucked up to the boss. After we dug into it, my client decided his dragons were Impostor Syndrome and Irrelevance. He discounted his inclusion in the CEO's succession plan by saying the Board wanted him, not the CEO. No matter how many external accolades he received (there were many), he shrugged them off. He'd graduated with distinction in law but said he'd just worked harder than anyone else. In his discomfort, he kept his CEO and colleagues at bay. He wanted inclusion in the inner circle but didn't engage. He also felt inferior to his peers and constantly worried about being irrelevant. (Brené Brown says the number one cause of shame at work is fear of irrelevance.)

In his book *Who Really Matters,* Art Kleiner talks about the power of the "core group." The book shares a story about a rising star who says the customer doesn't come first, they come eighth. He then points out which executives come before the customer. Kleiner's point is that the politically savvy focus on keeping the core group satisfied. Core groups aren't all bad: they can be focused on self-gain or the good of the organization (or both). Some group members aren't executives; they may be influential or have a unique talent.

They're viewed as good sounding boards and often selected for ad hoc committees. Understanding these dynamics helps you navigate politics and makes it easier to do your job. Equating all politics with the dark side isn't helpful. This misplaced altruism can lead to self-righteousness ("I'd never do that"). A refusal to engage is a bad political move.

Here's everything I know about organizational politics:

1. It's unavoidable.
2. It's a game you can play without losing your soul.
3. It's possible to navigate politics ethically.
4. You can influence with integrity.

Politics exist wherever more than one person is involved. It's present well beyond work: in families and community organizations, and even between friends. In the workplace, many think it's confined to the upper echelons, but it's not. People at every level play politics, ethically or not. Many of us respond by trying to avoid politics altogether. Yet navigating politics will enhance your ability to influence positive change and boost your career success.

Erin Burt, author of *Seven Career Killers*, writes, "Avoiding politics altogether is deadly for your career. Every workplace has an intricate system of power and you can—and should—work it to your advantage." People with positive political savvy competencies (social astuteness, interpersonal influence, networking ability, and sincerity) have better career prospects and tend to get promoted more.[41]

So what is it exactly? I like this definition: "Organizational politics refers to a variety of activities associated with the use of influence tactics to improve personal or organizational interests."[42] It's about:

- Recognizing politics exist
- Viewing politics as neutral: it's how you "play" that makes it good or bad
- Knowing the networks of relationships throughout your organization
- Learning how to navigate politics where you work
- Using influence to positively affect change

Overly political people have been likened to foxes—crafty and hard to trust. They have hidden agendas, curry favors, and aren't trusted. The under political can be naive and too trusting, and they don't understand the value of saving face. They're not usually part of the core group and may be underestimated. The sweet spot is somewhere in between: understand your organization's politics and navigate it with integrity and smarts. Politics drive how work gets done. Choosing not to play is a political move.

Let's add power

Power is inseparable from politics and holds negative connotations. Misuse of power. Corruption. Bad behavior. Withholding information. Julie Diamond, author of the excellent book *Power: A User's Guide*, says it's easy to become anti-power if we've had bad experiences. But we all have power of some kind, even if we don't think so. Think of the many different types of power:

- Majority – you look like the majority and enjoy privileges you're unaware of
- Referent power – you're connected to someone powerful and they listen to you so you influence them
- Positional power – related to your title and responsibilities
- Physical power – strong and fit people who exude health and/or physical beauty
- Presence – charisma, gravitas, noticed when you walk in a room or even when sitting quietly
- Moral power – people whose reputation is above reproach; who behave with integrity
- Intellect – very intelligent people
- Scarcity – you're good at something most people aren't
- Network power – people with strong relationships who are connected to diverse networks
- Wealth – ability to invest in causes and projects
- Unity – the power of many people who unite to fight for a cause or against injustice
- Belief in your ability to influence
- Sense of self-efficacy – believe you have the ability to figure out or deal with whatever comes your way
- Confidence in your opinions

Whatever your role is, you likely possess some type of power. Many coaching clients are uncomfortable with this idea. No matter what your power source is, it's important to think about how it affects how you're perceived as you navigate politics. Senior executives automatically enjoy power. It's therefore important to play politics as ethically as possible.

Adding influence to the mix

Politics involves influence. And no matter what job you occupy, you need to influence to get things done, whether it's convincing a colleague to meet a deadline or seeking approval for a project. The Center for Creative Leadership says there are four keys to influence:

1. Organizational intelligence (a.k.a. political savvy): understanding your company's formal and informal structures;
2. Team promotion: judiciously sharing your team's successes to create visibility;
3. Trust building; and
4. Leveraging networks.

The most important influence factor? You. The medium is the message. Do you have credibility? Are you perceived as worth listening to? Are you talking to people who are supporters of yours or neutral about you? Is anyone a Darth Vader? Adjust your influencing accordingly. A news flash for me was that I didn't always have to be the influencer. Sometimes it was best if I wasn't. In such cases, provide key influencers (formally or informally) with information and they'll do the rest.

Socializing an idea was foreign to me. I was a straight shooter and just said what I thought. However, it's a good strategy to consider who you should meet to obtain input and understand potential objections before you pitch your idea in a big meeting. Include some in the core group and other key influencers. Listen to their feedback and adjust your idea. If they influence others in the core group, acceptance of your idea will increase exponentially.

So back to my coaching client with the Impostor Syndrome and Irrelevant dragons. We worked on separating the facts (accomplished professional in a senior position who exceeded his goals every year, was in the CEO succession plan and racked up numerous awards) from his interpretations (impostor, irrelevant, one day away from being fired). He couldn't slay his dragons, but he did diminish their power. Then I had him complete a political savvy assessment, which revealed that he had fantastic personal integrity but didn't know the corporate buzz, wasn't influential, didn't see the need to save face during disagreements, and needed to expand his relationship network. He finally decided to improve in these areas. About six months later, he was proud to tell me that he felt he was "in" with the CEO and the core group. Even better, he'd accomplished this ethically.

> *"MASTERING YOURSELF IS TRUE POWER."*
> –Lao Tzu

KELLIE GARRETT

CHAPTER 12 WORKBOOK

ELECTRONIC VERSIONS OF ALL WORKBOOKS ARE AVAILABLE AT KELLIEGARRETT.CA

What's your view of political savvy? Do you think it's the way people get things done or is it unsavory?

How would you benefit from enhancing your political savvy? How is this related to leadership as a way of being?

Have you ever thought of yourself as someone with power? Jot down why or why not.

Now look at the power sources earlier in this chapter. What are yours?

What dragons do you have that might be impeding your ability to engage ethically in politics, embrace your power, and influence others?

How is your level of consciousness helping or hindering your performance in these areas?

Resources

If you're interested in understanding where you sit regarding:

- Political Savvy: check out Brandon Partners' inexpensive organizational savvy assessment, which generates a useful report: https://brandonpartners.com/organizational-savvy-self-assessment/
- Influence: find a coach who can administer the Psychometrics Influence Style Indicator.

Books

Exercising Influence, B. Kim Barnes

Influence: Gaining Commitment, Getting Results, Harold Scharlatt & Roland Smith

Survival of the Savvy: High-Integrity Political Tactics for Career and Company Success, Rick Brandon and Marty Seldman

The Secret Handshake: Mastering the Politics of the Business Inner Circle, Kathleen Kelly Reardon, 2001

CHAPTER 13: COACHING ISSUE – FEEDBACK

Giving and receiving feedback in a productive manner is important at work and in your personal life. It's also needed for effective self-coaching. You need input from others to coach yourself. This chapter shares the elements required to successfully handle feedback.

"A MACHINE DOESN'T PERFORM BASED ON WHAT IT THINKS ABOUT HOW YOU MAKE IT FEEL. PEOPLE DO. YOU NEED TO SEE HOW YOUR BEHAVIOR AFFECTS OTHERS WITH FEARLESS INTROSPECTION, FEEDBACK SEEKING AND COMMITTED EFFORTS TO BEHAVIORAL CHANGE TO POSITIVELY IMPACT OTHERS."

–Monique Valcour[43]

Feedback really is a gift, whether you agree with it or not. Perception is reality and you'll miss valuable data if you discount feedback. You may be thinking that your dragons are already very good at criticizing you. Why do you need to invite even more into your life? Well, if you're committed to demonstrating leadership or climbing that consciousness ladder, it's important to understand how you impact those around you. You can't be an effective leader if you don't understand how you're perceived. And you can't coach yourself without the benefit of feedback.

Most of us take criticism very hard. If you get defensive, you'll stop receiving it. Clinical psychologist Harriet Lerner urges, "Listen with the same passion that we wish to be heard." (OMG, that's hard.) Even if you're not very sensitive, it's tough to hear anything other than praise. Why? Because humans need connection. Cavemen needed belonging to survive. (Why don't they ever talk about cavewomen?) If they got kicked out of the cave, they were a dead caveperson. Like it or not, they worked hard to retain a seat by the fire. We're not that different today. Hearing we need to behave differently sparks a fear of rejection. If someone criticizes us, we may lose our spot in the cave. On top of that, our inner five-year-old rebels: *You're not the boss of me! Why should I listen to you?* If you're interested in enhancing your leadership behavior and your level of consciousness, you need to invite feedback and handle it well when you receive it.

How to embrace feedback

So how do we ground ourselves enough to positively embrace feedback? An analogy about brand testing is useful. Surveys and focus groups help you understand if your company is fulfilling its value proposition (i.e., what you're promising customers). When you hear that order fulfillment is unacceptably slow, you don't negate the feedback. You dig into the numbers to find out what's going on. How long is it taking to get orders to customers? If it doesn't live up to your brand promise, you add more customer fulfillment staff or make the order process more efficient. If you find out the turnaround time can't be shortened, you change what you're promising customers.

Feedback is a gift; it just doesn't feel like one. When you anticipate feedback, your body tenses up. You may flush, grit your teeth, or sweat. It's normal. If you notice these reactions, you can consciously relax your body by breathing. (I don't know about you, but every time I remember to breathe, I'm shocked by how little air I usually get.) You're then in a better position to signal your openness: "I value your opinion; what's on your mind?" The more welcoming you are, the more the other person will relax. They'll then provide the feedback in a more positive way.

When you hear feedback, it's instinctive to say, "Oh no, that's not what I meant!" Then you explain yourself. But this negates their experience. Refrain from explaining yourself and say something like "I'm sorry my actions impacted you that way. Tell me more." This takes accountability for the negative impact and signals that you're curious about whatever else they want to share with you.

How do you think the other person feels? Relief that you're taking feedback well. More openness because they feel heard. You don't have to agree with anything. You may not even regret what you did. But you can always be genuinely sorry that your impact wasn't positive. You can then ask for ideas on how to move forward. What would they like you to do differently next time? What do they commit to? Request their support on whatever would be helpful.

When the stakes are higher (e.g., during a performance review), the same principles apply. When you're receiving feedback, it's natural to get hurt and defensive. That doesn't help your case. Pretend you're a journalist interested in another viewpoint. Why do they think the quality wasn't enough? What does quality look like? When have you delivered what they consider high-quality work? What suggestions do they have to help you improve?

Now, let's turn to the home front

Those you love best witness you when you're not at your best. And giving each other feedback—honestly and fairly—helps your relationship flourish. Again, how we deliver it matters. Do you have a habit of berating your partner and not acknowledging what they do well? Do you think you do everything right? Are you so sensitive that you can't take anything but "you're terrific"?

My husband Jay and I are both on our second marriages. (This one seems to be sticking, twenty-four years in.) My first husband wouldn't allow arguing (although I snuck them in by following him around the house when he wouldn't engage). He said hurtful things are said that aren't forgotten during arguments. The one who said it doesn't remember but the other one does. Although wise, it meant we didn't resolve much. Jay and his first wife had the same dynamic. No fighting, no resolution.

When Jay and I became a couple, we wanted to address whatever cropped up. (Okay, I was the one who wanted it; he concurred.) But we didn't have the skills required to air very different opinions. We're both dramatic and emotional. Hashing out meant lashing out. We'd both get hurt and angry.

One would stomp off (Jay). The other would follow (me). We'd say more things. We actually *yelled* sometimes. Ugh. The problem? We didn't know how to fight productively. So we went to marriage counseling in the Napa Valley. (We figured we may as well drink great wine while learning how to argue.) We found the amazing psychologist John Grey, who spent three days locked up in a room with us. It was emotional and exhausting. We started with small things. We had to write about something that drove our partner nuts. We both correctly guessed the topics. Jay is immaculate and washes the kitchen floor every night. If I make a sandwich, he washes it again. I won't see any crumbs but he will. I feel like Pigpen from Peanuts. He knew that I wanted him to be more demonstrative. I'm uber affectionate (remember Never Enough Dragon?) and Jay felt he already showered me with affection. So we'd fight about it, when all I wanted was a hug.

John Grey gave us many wonderful tools. I noticed many of the same principles that I used in coaching:

- "How are you feeling?" . . . listening and showing empathy. Resisting urge to say how I'm feeling first.
- "What sparked how you're feeling?" . . . listening
- "What would you like to be different?" . . . more listening
- "If this happens again, how would you like us to handle it?" . . . even more listening. (Gawd, being a mature adult involves a lot of listening.)
- "Are you ready to hear my thoughts?"

Whether at work or at home, the other person needs to feel heard before they're in the mood to listen to you. When we think our feelings don't count, we tend to misbehave. (I used to beat issues to death.) If you're truly committed to leadership as a way of being, make sure that you start viewing feedback like breathing. It's necessary and you don't even think about it when you're used to it.

You can't slay your dragons if you remain stuck in your habitual ways of operating. You may not ever fall in love with feedback but seeking it will provide you with valuable fodder to ponder in your self-coaching sessions.

Turning the tables: delivering feedback

When you're the boss, trust is foundational to successful feedback. If the person in front of you wonders whether you have their best interests at heart, feedback won't land well. You signal trust in multiple ways—many of them unspoken. Do you give them time on your calendar and honor meetings as if they were with the CEO? Is your body language inclusive in meetings? Do you ask for their opinion? Do you remember their child broke their leg and ask after them? These small acts show they matter to you. When you're in a feedback situation, they'll be more receptive because they'll feel you have their back.

We often avoid giving feedback because it's uncomfortable. When someone disappoints you or fails to deliver, you think, *That guy isn't a team player . . . he's lazy . . . doesn't care . . . just doesn't get it.* You see behavior, assume you know why the other person acted a certain way, and react based on your assumptions. You avoid the tough conversation: *I'll just find a workaround . . . get somebody else to do the work . . . commiserate with someone else.*

Former FCC CHRO Greg Honey says, "As a leader, what right do I have to withhold anything that will help you learn, grow and ultimately star in your role? If I really care for you, I **must** give you the feedback, coaching, and information you need to flourish." So what gets in the way of providing difficult, challenging, growth-oriented feedback? Honey says, "It comes down to you. Your desire to remain comfortable. Thinking you don't want to hurt anyone. But the person you don't want to hurt is you. It may hurt your reputation. It may hurt their perception of you." The way to address this is to ensure the other person knows you have their back (see Chapter 9 on trust). This prevents them from questioning your motives and makes them receptive to feedback. You'll still feel uncomfortable, but you'll go for it because you want to help them grow.

No one likes receiving feedback. When someone asks if they can give us feedback, we brace ourselves. But strong leaders are proficient at giving and receiving feedback. Things left unsaid can fester and damage relationships. The key is to establish trust and norms for giving and receiving feedback. When a conversation goes sideways, the norms help the relationship recover. Reframing feedback as a conversation about seeking to understand each other better can help. Although people usually *intend* to do the right thing, impact often doesn't match intention. The only way to know what someone intended is to ask them—and the only way to let a person know their impact is to tell them.

How to give feedback effectively

The Center for Creative Leadership developed a great model for delivering feedback called Situation-Behavior-Impact (SBI). It's easy to follow and helps reduce defensiveness, and it's simple and direct: You capture and clarify the situation; describe the specific, observable behaviors; and explain the impact of the behavior.

1. **Situation**: Describe the specific situation in which the behavior occurred.
   - Avoid generalities, such as "last week," as that can lead to confusion.
   - *Example*: "This morning at the 11 a.m. team meeting..."

2. **Behavior**: Describe the actual, observable behavior.
   - Keep to the facts. Don't insert opinions or judgments.
   - *Example*: "You interrupted me while I was telling the team about the monthly budget" instead of "You were rude."

3. **Impact**: Describe the results of the behavior.
   - Because you're describing exactly what happened and explaining your true feelings (not passing judgment), the listener is more likely to absorb what you say. If the effect was positive, words like "happy" or "proud" help underscore the success of the behavior. If the effect of the behavior was negative, you can use words such as "troubled" or "worried."

- *Example*: "I was impressed when you addressed that issue without being asked" or "I felt frustrated when you interrupted me because it broke my train of thought."

The success of SBI is enhanced when the feedback, which is one-way, is followed by an inquiry about intent, which makes the conversation two-way. Asking about their intentions helps you understand what was behind their actions. This allows you to draw attention to the gap between intent versus impact. Example: "What were you hoping to accomplish with that?" or "What was going on for you?" When the person receiving feedback is asked about their intentions, they'll feel heard. This helps build trust and understanding. Simple solutions usually follow. Inquiring about intent is also where good coaching starts. When you inquire about intention, motivation, or what's behind an action, you've entered a coaching conversation.

To further the two-way conversation, you can ask additional questions, such as:

- What could I have done differently?
- Was there additional support that I could have provided?
- Is there any feedback you would like to give me?

Once you've completed your discussion, explore what you both pledge to do when (not if) a future misunderstanding or problem arises.

Providing feedback in a timely manner is a challenge for most of my coaching clients. They don't want to be unkind and they don't want to be uncomfortable. Brené Brown says,

"Clear is kind. Unclear is unkind." (So true.) The best way to effectively share feedback is by tuning into how hard it is to receive it yourself. It's completely natural to get defensive (remember the cavemen). We don't like being criticized. Our dragons are already doing a number on us. We're also filtering whatever's said through trust. Does the person delivering feedback have our back or are they trying to make us look bad? Finally, we want to avoid feeling shamed. It takes discipline and maturity to view every kind of feedback as useful. We don't have to agree, and we don't have to act on it.

KELLIE GARRETT

CHAPTER 13 WORKBOOK

ELECTRONIC VERSIONS OF ALL WORKBOOKS ARE AVAILABLE AT KELLIEGARRETT.CA

When you receive feedback, how do you generally react? What's going on inside (emotions, thoughts, body, e.g., flushing)? What's visible outside (do you get quiet, aggressive, upset)?

....

....

Thinking about the different levels of consciousness, what do you need to grow in this area so that you can embrace feedback with curiosity and deliver it with empathy?

....

....

How might you demonstrate leadership as a way of being vis-à-vis receiving feedback?

....

....

What dragons are at play when you receive feedback? How might you combat them?

....

....

Common dragons

- Not Enough Dragon
- Perfecto Dragon (perfectionism)
- People Pleaser Dragon (need to be liked)
- Shame Dragon

Now, thinking of providing feedback:

How might you take into account your own reactions to receiving feedback when you provide it to others?

What practices will you adopt when providing feedback?

Resources

David Rock's SCARF Model: Using Neuroscience to Work Effectively with Others, Mindtools. https://www.mindtools.com/akswgc0/david-rocks-scarf-model

Find the Coaching in Criticism, Sheila Heen and Douglas Stone, *Harvard Business Review*, January-February 2014. https://hbr.org/2014/01/find-the-coaching-in-criticism

Use Situation-Behavior-Impact (SBI)™ to Understand Intent, Center for Creative Leadership. https://www.ccl.org/articles/leading-effectively-articles/closing-the-gap-between-intent-vs-impact-sbii/

Two-Thirds of Managers are Uncomfortable Communicating with Employees, Lou Solomon, *Harvard Business Review*, March 9, 2016. https://hbr.org/2016/03/two-thirds-of-managers-are-uncomfortable-communicating-with-employees

COMMON COACHING THEMES – WRAP-UP

The topics covered in Chapters 8 to 13 covered the following themes, which I've noticed in coaching scores of clients:

- Self-awareness and self-management (emotional intelligence)
- Trust building and rebuilding
- Confidence
- Mental toughness
- Political savvy and power
- Giving and receiving feedback

If one of these subjects resonates, use the corresponding chapter as input to coaching yourself. If none apply to you or something else is more pressing, hopefully the overview of these topics will help you decide what you want to tackle in your self-coaching.

PART IV

THE COACHING PROCESS AND SELF-COACHING WITH THE DRAGONS MODEL

CHAPTER 14: JOLTS OF AWAKENING – THE COACHING PROCESS

It's useful to understand the various components of coaching and its success factors. This chapter explains the coaching process used by professional coaches, which forms the basis of the DRAGONS self-coaching model.

"THE OPPONENT WITHIN ONE'S HEAD IS MORE FORMIDABLE THAN THE ONE ON THE OTHER SIDE OF THE NET."

–Timothy Gallwey, tennis coach

The hero's journey is a great metaphor for coaching. It goes like this: after leading an ordinary life, the protagonist battles multiple ordeals and returns transformed.

Now, let's shift to your life:

You're trucking along when you realize something isn't working. It may be dramatic (you're fired, divorcing, or receive a diagnosis). Or you gradually realize you're unhappy, stuck, or something's not right. You stuff feelings down and try to soldier on. But the unease doesn't disappear. You think, *This sucks and something needs to change, and oh crap, that something might be me.* This is when your quest begins. You find a coach or therapist. If it's coaching, you decide on your goals and examine your current reality. You gain awareness of your patterns and start to see your part to play in things. You try different techniques that you've noodled through with your coach. You feel discouraged, encouraged, discouraged. If you're lucky, you have an aha that transforms how you see things and ignites change.

My best coaching experiences always jolted me awake with an aha. *So that's why I'm stuck!* **Now** *I see what needs to be different.* I felt both highly conscious and—heroic. This fueled a desire to change. Now, that short word contains volumes. Wanting to change and actually changing consists of what feels like a hero's journey. Awareness and desire is just the start. Remember Kegan and Lahey's work on immunity to change (referenced in Chapter 2)? You must also identify your blind spots, deep-rooted assumptions, beliefs, mindsets, and competing commitments—many of which may be unconscious. Once you've identified all this, you're in a position to rewire how you operate. Easy, right?

Coaches help you navigate this tough terrain. They follow a model to guide the process of coaching. Most coaching models are based on the GROW model, developed by Sir John Whitmore.[44] GROW stands for Goals – Reality – Options – Way forward:

GOAL: The coach helps you identify what you want to achieve as a result of being coached.

REALITY: An exploration of your current situation. What's going on for you that's related to your Goal? What's working? What's not? A series of awareness questions, exercises, and assessments help you understand your patterns of thought, emotions, and behavior.

OPTIONS: The coach helps you generate ideas to reach your goal. This occurs through various questions and techniques. If you're stuck, your coach may ask if you need additional ideas.

WAY FORWARD: You decide what actions and mindset shifts are required to achieve your goal. This often includes sources of support.

Coaching isn't linear

What's described above is straightforward. It's anything but when humans are involved. The coaching journey more often goes like this:

You're asked what goals you have for the coaching engagement. What do you want to be different? You may be clear or unsure. If it's the latter, your coach helps you explore until you land on what resonates.

You move on to the current situation. What's working? What isn't? You explore various issues and behaviors. You may wallow, thinking everything's your fault. Or you externalize blame. You have an aha or two and it starts to dawn on you that the real issue is you. (Not a fun aha.)

You uncover some inner dragons: a mixture of your inner critic, limiting beliefs, and protective strategies. Dragons show up everywhere we go, not just at work or at home. (This is annoying. You are the common denominator in all your issues.)

You experiment with doing things differently. It isn't easy, or it downright sucks. You try another way. You see progress.

You create new problems (e.g., you react to others differently and they're not used to it. Very demoralizing.) You go back to old habits and ways of thinking. You realize those don't work either and get frustrated. You blame your coach or yourself. Maybe you don't have what it takes to nuke the damned dragons.

You get in your own way again, so you start trying new behaviors, habits, and mindsets. You discover you can't conquer all your dragons. Rats. Familiarizing yourself with the unbeatable dragons helps you learn coping mechanisms. *(I see you, Dragon, but you don't get to run the show. Go sit in the corner while I handle this meeting.)*

Suddenly or slowly, you experience a new way of thinking and being. You look at everything through a new lens. Nothing has changed except you. This expands your level of consciousness. You transform, which isn't the same thing as never having another problem.

All this to say that reaching your coaching goal isn't linear. And not everyone experiences a major "aha." But most clients obtain insights that alter how they think and behave.

Here are common issues I've observed after countless hours of coaching:

- The driven executive gets high-quality results but doesn't see how she's negatively impacting employee morale.
- The middle manager goes from being a peer to a boss, who knows how to be friends with colleagues but doesn't know how to hold them accountable for performance.

- A director who demoralizes staff because he micromanages every aspect of their projects.
- The rising star whose progress is derailed because she won't engage in office politics, viewing them as dirty.
- The uber-bright director with no patience for anyone around him because they aren't fast enough and don't get it.
- The highly accomplished person who lacks confidence, feels like an impostor, and holds themselves back.

Since you can't separate the human who goes to work from who they really are, coaching inevitably involves the whole person. The driven executive may be negatively impacting people at home as well as work. The middle manager notices he's a people pleaser outside the office. The accomplished professional is ticked that her family doesn't share her high standards, so she does everything herself. The rising star is self-righteous where she volunteers, not just at work. The impatient director ignores personal relationships.

Even when people *want* to change something, there's a tendency to cling to habitual ways of being. As part of the coaching process, the client is asked how a pattern of behavior they say they want to change is serving them. The client may or may not know in that moment. It usually takes a while to uncover the answer.

Some common reasons include:

- My work is excellent and I know how to get results. I don't know how to get results through others, so I don't

delegate. It will take too long to teach my staff to do what I can do. I have to keep doing everything myself.
- I'm a direct person, a straight shooter. Some people find that overly blunt. But I don't want to stop being authentic, so that's their problem.
- I don't do politics. I think they're unsavory at best and downright unethical sometimes. I refuse to play the game.
- I know how to be pessimistic. I don't want to be disappointed. I'm always waiting for the other shoe to drop.

Changing these mindsets or any others is difficult because humans don't like change. We like to feel safe so we keep doing what we do, even when it doesn't serve us. We look for data that validates our thoughts, habits, and beliefs (confirmation bias). We're comfortable with what we know. Why choose to stand on rocky ground? Because if you want to be the best you can be—choosing leadership behaviors at work and at home—you need to let go of your version of truth and really listen to other perspectives. This is the doorway to growth. Being suspicious of what you think you know helps open your mind. Coaching invites you to change and then learn how to sustain it.

Even if you hire a magnificent coach, coaching doesn't always work. There are lots of reasons why, including:
- Failure to identify the real dragon
- Unsure about the desired future state
- Trying to change too much at once
- Avoiding uncomfortable feelings

- Premature identification of solution
- Unwilling to surrender to not knowing
- Not looking in the mirror and owning your part
- Wedded to habitual ways of being
- Lack of sustained commitment
- Victim mentality: externalizing blame

When coaching works, it's a game changer

Aha! I get it! New thoughts, emotions, behaviors, and reactions kick-start a virtuous spiral that can affect every aspect of your life.

Leslie Rohonczy, a wonderfully wise leadership coach, author, musician, and artist (a Renaissance woman) says, "As a coach, I've been so privileged to walk alongside people and witness the profound transformations possible within this confidential, judgment-free relationship. Coaching is a powerful 'consciousness accelerator' because it puts proven, practical techniques into action, to help people identify barriers, manage uncomfortable emotions, tame inner critics, overcome limiting beliefs, and cultivate new awareness and skills for lasting results. When people feel really stuck, coaching can help to alleviate their suffering and illuminate new possibilities, and that's a game changer."

Coaches use various ways to help you identify your desired state and the goals to reach it. We then work to raise awareness regarding patterns and behaviors that are preventing you from attaining the goal. Coaches don't tell you what to do. We hold you as capable and competent. As Parker Palmer says, this involves active listening and asking questions "that help others hear their inner wisdom more clearly."[45]

At the beginning of an engagement, I always ask the client: "If you had a great coaching experience, what would you walk away with?" Typical answers include, "I would . . .

- know what my next career step is."
- be more confident."
- be able to handle criticism better."
- be more politically savvy."
- communicate my ideas with more clarity."
- have tough conversations with my staff."
- manage stress better."
- be more productive and work fewer hours."

A coach can't provide the magic potion that will get you to these desired end states. A coach *can* help you uncover what's standing in your way. Often, it's your dragons within—beasts consisting of your inner critic, limiting beliefs, and protective behaviors. Identifying your dragons and how they prevent you from reaching your goal is at the heart of coaching.

What all coaching models have in common is the decision about the goals, exploration of the current reality, sifting through options, and deciding what course to take. Coaching may help you to address a relatively minor desired change or ignite transformation.

Understanding how coaching works is foundational to learning how to coach yourself. We'll get into that in the next chapter.

CHAPTER 15: SELF-COACHING CHECKLIST

You don't go on a long road trip without checking your vehicle's condition. Ditto for you.

- If you have a mental health issue, don't coach yourself. Find a therapist.
- If you're struggling with major challenges, now is not the right time for self-coaching. You may wish to find a professional coach instead.

Note: If you uncover some difficult issues during your self-coaching journey, know when to stop. You may need a break and/or need to get help.

Remember, it takes courage to seek help.

Start your engines! Learning to coach yourself is incredibly helpful as a stand-alone practice or a supplement to professional coaching. Just like a coach adheres to certain principles and structure, self-coaching benefits from these too. Coaches follow a coaching model (from goal identification to practices that will sustain change), engage in active listening, ask powerful questions, challenge your thinking, and draw out your inner wisdom. Each coaching session is followed by reflection and exercises; for example, noticing your patterns and reactions. When coaching sticks, it's because you shed unproductive beliefs and behaviors. You leave coaching equipped with practices to sustain a new way of being.

Here's what you need to know before you start coaching yourself.

Self-coaching program length and timing

When hiring a coach, you agree on program length and meeting frequency. An initial engagement usually lasts six months. Most clients opt for a biweekly meeting schedule. Others prefer every three to four weeks. With less frequency, you lose momentum. Decide how long you want to coach yourself on a particular issue. Think about when you'll carve out the time. It might be once a week or every couple of weeks. Whatever it is, setting appointments with yourself will help you to get traction.

Treat yourself with unconditional positive regard

A coach holds space for clients from a stance of "unconditional positive regard," a term coined by psychologist Carl Rogers. This means that nothing the client does will destroy the coach's regard for them. Since it's difficult to face your dragons and your part to play, it's important to treat *you* with unconditional positive regard. It may be helpful to create a mantra or sentence to use if (or when) you start beating yourself up. In Kathryn Stockett's book *The Help*, the maid ends up mothering her employer's neglected child. Whenever something hard happens, the maid reminds her, "You is smart. You is kind. You is important." It's useful to create some variety of this for yourself. Mine is KARMA: Kellie, all reaction means angst. When I start hearing criticism from my dragons (or anyone else), this simple mantra reminds me to step back and not react with negative self-talk. Here are some ideas for you:

- "You exceed your goals every year. You can deal with this."
- "This sounds like a fact, but it's not."
- "You are not your thoughts."
- "Thank you, Dragon, for trying to protect me, but I'm releasing you now."

Adopt a stance of unconditional positive regard and know how you'll unhook yourself when triggered (e.g., with your mantra) before you start coaching yourself.

Know your coaching model

Just like coaches select a coaching model (usually from the school where they received training), you need one to coach yourself. I've created the DRAGONS self-coaching model for you to follow, which is covered in the next chapter.

Hire your higher self as your coach

This is about learning to access your inner wisdom and trust it. Each step of the DRAGONS self-coaching model involves tuning into your higher self. If you're not sure how to tune in, I recommend practicing before you embark on self-coaching. Chapter 3 is devoted to this topic and will provide you with ideas.

Self-coaching tips

Great coaches ask powerful questions. It's a hard skill to master and even tougher when coaching yourself. You have habitual ways of asking yourself questions and talking to yourself. Questioning your questions needs to be part of your self-coaching process.

But questions are only part of the equation. As Master Certified Coach Dr. Marcia Reynolds says, "the key [coaching] competency isn't powerful questions; the foundation of coaching is presence. The coach needs to be present to the whole person and his or her experience. This includes acknowledging the emotions the client is feeling in the moment and recognizing the energy shifts that are occurring (a person can feel excited and resentful in one sentence!)."[46] Since you're coaching you, remember that being fully present to yourself, acknowledging your emotions, and recognizing your energy shifts are important, even more important than trying to figure out the right question.

The questions you ask and how you ask them will drive the direction your self-coaching takes. Consider the following tips.

1. Balance subjectivity with objectivity

In self-coaching, your job is to balance subjectivity (easy, because it's your experience, your feelings, your thoughts) with objectivity—stepping back to examine your experience. An ability to be objective is essential to self-coaching and very difficult. It doesn't negate your subjective experience, which also holds valuable data.

Objectivity entails examining your experience as if it weren't yours, including what you're thinking and feeling. This detachment provides a different vantage point. When someone yells at you in a meeting, your subjective experience might be hurt and anger. Your narrative could be "He doesn't like me. He's out to get me. I didn't do anything wrong." When looking at the same situation objectively, you'd focus on the facts. You presented something. Your peer asked several questions about the presentation. You answered them. They raised their voice. There's no dislike, vendetta, or judgment. Stepping back allows you to generate more perspectives about what happened, which will spark ideas regarding future thoughts and actions.

Other objective questions to ask yourself: What happened? When? What did I notice? What assumptions am I making? What happened as a result? Meditation and mindfulness practices are very helpful with objectivity. The goal is to examine questions from a stance of detachment and non-judgment. (Some of these practices are covered in Chapter 3.)

Looking at the same situation from both the subjective and objective provides you with rich insights. You'll have a better sense of your part to play in each situation and coach yourself on how you'll handle a similar one.

2. Think of someone who asks good questions—in meetings or in your personal life. Pretend they are asking the question. How would they pose it to you?

3. Replace "why" with "what"

Researcher Tasha Eurich says that "why" questions are ineffective: "*Why* don't I trust this person?" or "*Why* am

I so upset?" Because you can't access your unconscious thoughts, motives, and feelings, your answers "feel true but are often wrong." "Why" questions can also lead to negative rumination.

Asking "what" questions keep you more objective and future focused. Replace "Why am I so upset?" with "What situations tend to upset me and are there any commonalities to those?" Eurich's findings echo research conducted by psychologists J. Gregory Hixon and William Swann, who concluded that "Thinking about why one is the way one is may be no better than not thinking about oneself at all."

4. Be curious and neutral, not critical and negative

Coaches don't embed a judgment (negative or positive) in their questions.

Curious and neutral: "What led up to this situation?" "What do you need to move forward?"

Negative: "What makes you think you can do this?" "Why do you always make mistakes?"

Critical questions don't generate growth: Curious questions are helpful: *What can I learn from this setback?* or *I notice I'm hard on myself—what if I stopped criticizing myself so harshly?*

5. Don't use "always" or "never"

Marriage counselors recommend this. When someone else says you always or never do something, you discount whatever comes next. Your mind refutes it, coming up with instances where it did or didn't happen. Unfortunately, when you talk to yourself, it's the opposite. You buy into the narrative that you "always" screw up, which isn't true. Neither is "You *never* do anything right." Talk to yourself the way you deserve to be spoken to.

6. Listen to more than your mind

Many of us attempt to solve things intellectually. Your cognitive capacity is wonderful but limiting when it's your main knowledge source. Emotions send powerful signals that inform your thoughts. It just happens so quickly that you don't realize an emotion preceded your thoughts. Enlist your emotions, body, intuition, and other ways of knowing (including your higher self) to supplement the workings of your beautiful mind. These provide valuable inputs to coaching yourself. Some ways of getting out of your head include walking meditation, drawing, or stream of consciousness journaling. (See Chapter 3 for more ideas.)

7. Be specific

Coaching involves examining an issue and then coming up with actions to address it. Be specific (e.g., *When you did x, you said it didn't turn out so great. What did you learn from this? Based on this learning, what specific actions could you take?*)

8. Seek external inputs

To be effective, self-coaching can't occur in a vacuum. That's why you need to seek varied information sources. These include your Darth Vaders, neutral folks, and your fans.

What matters is themes. Do all three of these groups have similar perceptions about you? That's worth pondering at your next self-coaching session. (See Chapter 13 on feedback.)

9. Pattern identification

Note any patterns to your questions and answers. I noticed the word "they" cropped up all the time when I thought about trust. It was all "they" and no "me." Recognizing the pattern made me realize I was externalizing blame. That led to a whole host of helpful self-coaching questions.

When you're coaching yourself, step back after asking questions. Look at your journal. Can you identify a pattern in your entries? *Hmm. I sound like nothing ever works and there's no way to change what I want to be different. I don't want to be negative.* Pattern identification is very important in coaching.

10. Understand how people change

Remember that awareness and desire aren't enough to sustain change. Refer to Chapter 2's resources on change and consider downloading the free Immunity to Change map.

11. Notice synchronicity

Once you start looking for red cars, you see them everywhere. Once you start seeking answers from your higher self, you'll find synchronicity. For example: You decide to coach yourself on life balance. You notice how some people achieve balance and others seem to be in a hot mess. You see opportunities where you didn't before. Notice what keeps showing up once you've sent your question/plea to the universe and/or your higher self.

So now you're equipped with some principles to use in coaching yourself. Here's what you do next.

At Every Session

Trust yourself

A good coach builds trust and sustains it throughout the engagement. Self-coaching requires that you trust yourself. (Why is that hard?) Trust that you already have inner wisdom. It's there in the form of your higher self. And don't forget unconditional positive regard.

Be present and kind to yourself

Before a coaching session, I review notes from previous meetings and then sit in silence to ground myself. I hold my client in my heart and wish for their well-being. I also clear my mind so I can be fully present. Do this before you have a coaching session with yourself. Hold yourself in your own heart. Make a wish for your well-being. (You may feel emotional, even brought to tears. It's so rare that we turn warmth inward. Enjoy it.) Put your phone away. Devote this time to you.

Focus self-coaching on your goal

It's tempting to go down a rabbit hole that's unrelated to your coaching goal. That's okay if it helps you realize the goal should change. Usually, it's a distraction. When you go off on a tangent in a coaching session, your coach refocuses you to discuss what's relevant to your coaching goal. When coaching yourself, pay attention to meandering thoughts. Focus your questions and musings through the lens of your goal.

Choose how you'll keep track

When you meet with a coach, it's useful to jot a few notes down and refer to them between sessions. With self-coaching, you're meeting with you. Choose how you'll track progress. Buy a journal that's devoted to your self-coaching. Make voice recordings or use an electronic journal. Pick whatever works for you.

First Self-Coaching Session

Draft your goals

The first session between a coach and a client is devoted to drafting goals for the coaching engagement. This provides focus throughout the program. Some common goals may get your juices flowing:

- Conquer impostor syndrome and grow confidence
- Reduce stress and increase balance
- Be ready for a promotion
- Change a reputation
- Increase influence
- Build and rebuild trust

Take a stab at drafting one clear goal for your self-coaching. You can tackle multiple ones later.

Note: Sometimes the coaching goals change after an aha or two. This is a-okay.

Subsequent coaching sessions

Use the principles from earlier in this chapter and some of the coaching questions on the following pages.

You're ready to rumble!

CHAPTER 15 WORKBOOK

ELECTRONIC VERSIONS OF ALL WORKBOOKS ARE AVAILABLE AT KELLIEGARRETT.CA

What's in it for me to coach myself?

Initial thoughts about my self-coaching topic:

CHAPTER 16: DRAGONS SELF-COACHING MODEL

This chapter provides a structure for you to follow as you embark on coaching yourself. It concludes with a template to help you put your self-coaching into practice. Don't rush this chapter. There's lots to explore.

The International Coaching Federation defines coaching as "partnering with clients in a thought-provoking and creative process that inspires them to maximize their personal and professional potential. The process of coaching often unlocks previously untapped sources of imagination, productivity and leadership."[47] While you don't have a coach as a partner, I suggest that you keep this definition top of mind as you coach yourself.

As covered in Chapter 14, coaching models generally consist of these elements:

- defining a goal—what you want to achieve as a result of being coached
- exploring your current situation—what's working and what isn't
- embarking on a journey of awareness that includes pattern identification, beliefs, habits of thought, and reaction. It may also entail the use of assessments.
- generating options to pursue that will address what you've learned

- selecting actions to reach your goal, based on your insights

This sounds incredibly straightforward but it's not. Coaches use the framework above as a map. A map provides you with an overview of the territory you'll cover. It only hints at the richness of each stop along the way.

I created my own model as a framework to guide self-coaching. I named the model DRAGONS because they affect so many coaching clients. Remember, dragons consist of inner critics, limiting beliefs, and protective behaviors that don't serve you. The model outlines the steps to follow as you embark on coaching yourself.

Different: What you want to be different and what dragons are involved, then determining a goal to get there.

Reality: Exploring your current situation and what you've tried so far.

Awareness: Awareness of self, patterns, reactions

Aha's: flashes of insight

Galvanize: Get excited into taking action

Obstacles: What may get in the way of achieving your goal: internal and external

New: New way of being, behaving, and believing and actions to sustain momentum

Higher Self: Guidance from your higher self, and aligning new actions and ways of being with higher self

Although the "S" in DRAGONS is listed last, I recommend tuning into your higher self for guidance at each step. For example, the first step (the "D" in DRAGONS) is about what you want to be different (e.g., I want more balance.) This step also includes figuring out the related dragon. You may not know this up front. Answer the questions and then sit with them for a few days or weeks. This is when you'll access your higher self. Consider using the practices from Chapter 3 to do this. If your higher self is best accessed while walking, take balance along with you. Don't ask for an answer. Be present with the weather, the path, the sky, the birds. You realize, yes, it's balance. Or it's still fuzzy. That's okay. Hold the topic of balance in your head, heart, and body, and go through your days. You may realize it's not balance after all. It's different work. Your higher self may reveal you're tired because you're pursuing the wrong career. Then what you want to be different isn't balance, but a new job. What's holding you back is Impostor Syndrome Dragon.

What if you can't find your higher self? That's perfectly fine. Don't force it. Answer the questions in the DRAGONS model. Notice any emotions that come up for you at each step: excitement, boredom, frustration, sadness, etc. Now listen to your body. Is it relaxed or tight? Allow these data points to inform your cognitive answers. Before long, you may find your way in. Your higher self is already there, whether you see it or not.

Learn to love the questions themselves

The following chart includes questions you can ask yourself at each stage of the DRAGONS model. The Appendix contains many additional questions you can consider. But a note of caution: asking yourself questions tends to be a cognitive exercise. To access messages from your feelings, body, and higher self, choose an idea or two from Chapter 3 and commit to practicing them. Try integrating these with how you live your life. When you feel connected to all of you—not just your magnificent brain—it's easier to understand what all of you needs and wants. Finally, it's more important to sit with what arises than coming up with the perfect answer. As Rainer Maria Rilke wrote in *Letters to a Young Poet*,

> "Be patient toward all that is unsolved in your heart and try to love the questions themselves, like locked rooms and like books that are now written in a very foreign tongue. Do not now seek the answers, which cannot be given you because you would not be able to live them. And the point is, to live everything. Live the questions now. Perhaps you will then gradually, without noticing it, live along some distant day into the answer."

D	**Different & Dragons**	**What do I want to be different? What dragon is holding me back?**	**Questions to ponder**
Define what you want to be different – use outcome-oriented questions. Connect what you want to be different to one of your dragons. If you aren't sure what your dragons are, that's okay. They'll show up. ☺ Set your coaching goal, which should include what you want to be different as well as the related dragon.			What do I want to be different? When things are different, what will my future look like? What's in it for me to change? Is a dragon behind my desire for change? How does this dragon drive my behavior? Does my higher self have any guidance on my desired future state, dragon, or goal?
R	**Reality**	**Understand current reality**	**Questions**
This is about understanding what's going on for you in the current situation. Jot down facts, feelings, and interpretations.			What's going on? First, stick to the facts and then add feelings and interpretations. What's working about the current situation? What's not working about staying where I am? What gives me energy? What drains it? What's causing me stress? What have I tried to change so far? What guidance does my higher self have regarding my current reality?
A	**Awareness & Aha's**		**Questions**
Discover patterns in my beliefs, behaviors, and reactions. Aha's from Awareness Note: Organizations identify strengths, weaknesses, opportunities, and threats (SWOT). To gain awareness, try to "SWOT yourself." A strength overplayed is a weakness. An opportunity may also be a threat.			What patterns can I identify in my beliefs, behaviors, and reactions? What's my part to play in what's happening? When I'm at my best, what am I like? When I'm not at my best, what am I like? What circumstances do I view as unchangeable? Why? What level of consciousness do I operate from? Where would I like to be? How might I shed my attachment to being smart, liked, or in control? If I were to view leadership as a way of being, what am I doing well vs. not? Does my higher self have anything to add regarding my self-awareness exploration?

G	Galva-nize	Excited to take action!	Questions
Galvanize means to shock or excite into action. This is about gearing up to try something new. You're clear on what you want to be different, you've examined your current reality, and you've had aha's sparked by greater awareness of your patterns, triggers, and reactions. You're ready to galvanize! This step is shorter but often needs revisiting. When you lose your mojo, remind yourself what galvanized you. So then the model looks like DRAGOGOGONS. ☺ Galvanize might be the most important element of this model. Without feeling galvanized to action and then sustaining that feeling, the rest is academic. When you feel the shock or excitement that galvanizes action, seize the day and head to the Obstacle course.			What excites me about reaching my goal? How will I sustain my motivation? If I've tried before without success, what is different this time? When I experience a setback, how will I talk to myself? What will I do when I feel discouraged to stay the course?
O	Obstacles	What could get in your way	Questions
Consider what might block you from attaining your goal. Choose a few strategies to contend with the obstacles. Ask your higher self about the obstacles and strategies you've identified.			What might prevent me from reaching my goal? What other obstacles do I expect to encounter? How might my dragon(s) stand in the way of reaching my goal? What strategies do I need to combat my dragon? Are there ways I self-sabotage beyond what my dragon does? How do I get in my own way now and how might I get in my own way in the future? How might I surmount these obstacles? When I experience a setback or major challenges, what is my typical reaction and how will I replace it with something productive?

KELLIE GARRETT

N	**New**	**New way of being, behaving, and believing**	**Questions**
Describe the behaviors and beliefs that will help you consistently demonstrate what you've decided will be different and sustain your goals. New way of being: choose practices to embed your new behaviors. Tune into higher self for any related messages.			Where do I want to be a year from now with respect to my goal? What do I need to get there? (e.g., beliefs, behaviors) What are my next steps? What's one action I can take to move me toward my goal? Capabilities: Do I know how to do this new thing? If not, can I outline what skills I need to support my ability to change? What practices will I adopt to support my new way of being, behaving, and believing? What kind of support will help me? How will I stay accountable to myself? How might I deal with what I can't change? What does my higher self have to say?
S	**Self**	**Alignment between my higher self and my words and actions**	**Questions**
Your higher self is a powerful source of guidance and is foundational to self-coaching. It's at your center, where you're the most you. It knows your gifts, your flaws, your mistakes, your cares. It's all-accepting. This is about tuning into the wisdom of your higher self and ensuring that the new actions and ways of being you choose are aligned with this center.			What guides my life? What is deeply true for me? When I am in tune with my soul or higher self, what am I thinking, feeling, doing? How are these related to the coaching goal and actions I have chosen?

DRAGONS Self-coaching example:

This example should help you to complete your own DRAGONS self-coaching chart. Remember, it's not just about answering the questions from your head. Use your feelings, thoughts, body wisdom, and higher self to answer. You can draft a few answers and then spend a few days just sitting with them, using your higher self practices from Chapter 3. Or you can do it in reverse. Think only of what you want to be different and use your practices to obtain wider wisdom that your brain has. Then revisit what you've written and alter it to reflect what you learned in the intervening days.

D	Different & Dragons	What do you want to be different?
	Define what you want to be different. When things are different, what will that future state look like?	I want balance in my life I'd work 45 hours a week, not 55 I'll have more time for my family, exercise, and even leisure. I won't feel stressed out all the time.
	Connect what you want to be different to one of your dragons. (if you don't know, just write "not sure.") Where did this dragon come from? How does this dragon drive your behavior?	I think it's Dumbo the Dragon (not smart enough). No matter how many accolades I get, I never feel good enough. It's like compliments don't stick to me. My parents. Although that seems like a cop-out because I'm 41! Nothing was ever good enough. Even straight As. I think it's Never Good Enough. Dumbo is a subset. It drives insecurity, perfectionism (nothing's ever good enough), and overwork.
	Set your coaching goal, which should include what you want to be different as well as the related dragon.	Goal: To lead a balanced life, which will mean working fewer hours and believing I'm smart enough.
	Reality	**Understand your current reality**
	\multicolumn{2}{l|}{I usually work 55 hours a week – even that's not enough. I'm pretty good at getting stuff done quickly, but I spend almost all day in meetings, so I can't get other work done until evenings or weekends. I don't have enough people to delegate some work I shouldn't be doing. I don't have time for friends or exercise or hobbies. Even when I'm not working, I'm thinking about work or even dreaming about it!}	

KELLIE GARRETT

Awareness & Aha's	Awareness of self, patterns, reactions, and Aha's: flashes of insight

When do you shine? When are you at your best?
I shine when I'm working with my direct reports or with the team, listening, coaching, pushing them to do what they don't think they can do, and cheering them on when they accomplish something.
At home, I shine when I'm playing anything with my kids – a game, swimming, basketball. Playing guitar and singing with them. I take my husband's needs into account (i.e., it's not all about me).

What conditions cause this?
At work: Having enough time to be patient enough to coach and not be directive.
At home: Having enough time to drop everything to play with the kids.

When are you at your worst?
When I'm very stressed. I stop having one-on-one meetings, put my head down and work. At home: I'm impatient with the kids and bark at them. I get annoyed with my husband and don't listen to what he needs.

Do you know what causes this response? Too many conflicting priorities. Exhaustion.

What are your three top strengths? Smart, patient, extroverted

What does each strength look like when it's overdone?
Smart: I think I'm the only one with the right answer.
Patient: I feel taken advantage of. I lack boundaries to say "that's enough."
Extroverted: I can take up too much room, talk too much.

What are your gifts? How are they related to the dragon? (Throttle, strength overplayed is a flaw.)
Smart, good with people, creative, fast.

I don't know how to get everything done at work. There really aren't enough hours in the day. But other reasons prevent balance: I say yes to everything. I have FOMO. I feel like nothing's ever good enough – quality of work, my response in a meeting could have been better, I don't spend enough time with my staff, with my kids, with my husband. That's not really Dumbo the Dragon. More like Never Good Enough Dragon.

How is what's going on right now serving you?
It's not! Are you crazy?

How is what's occurring not serving you?
I'm exhausted and stressed. I'm not looking after myself. I use wine to relax. I feel like all I do is work and look after kids. I'm losing my sense of humor. I feel like I'm on a hamster wheel and I can't get off.

How are others causing this predicament?
My boss springs things on me at the last minute. Even though my department pushes through a lot of work, I don't get any recognition from my boss. I don't get material with enough lead time.

What situations cause your current reality?
Too many meetings
Not enough senior people reporting to me who can do the kind of work I can
What's your part to play in what's not working?
I'm not good at saying no. I don't want to overburden my people so I don't delegate enough. I don't set boundaries between work and my personal life.

What is your habitual reaction to the current situation?
Work extra hours. Drink wine. Complain to my husband and coworkers. Drop anything that isn't related to the kids

Awareness & Aha's	Awareness of self, patterns, reactions, and Aha's: flashes of insight

Do you have this reaction to any other kinds of situations?
Not that I can think of

Are any of your strengths contributing to this situation? (Smart, patient, extroverted)
Patient: I feel taken advantage of

Are any of your flaws contributing to this situation?
Perfectionism: nothing is ever good enough: I have trouble letting go of things, always think of one more thing to add to polish whatever I'm doing.
Lack of boundaries: don't say "that's enough"

What level of consciousness do I operate from? Where would I like to be?
I'd like to say it's at the creative/self-authored level, but I think it's often below: the reactive/socialized mind.
I'm in the creative mode when I'm listening to my team members: coaching, inspiring, and celebrating successes. Also, when I'm fully present with my kids and husband, and take their needs into account.

I'd like to consistently remain at the creative level. I care too much about what others think and that contributes to the boundary issue, perfectionism, and probably a host of other challenges.

Do I have an attachment to being smart, liked or in control?
Liked and in control. Liked is related to boundaries and control is linked to perfectionism. Both impair my ability to find balance.

If I were to view leadership as a way of being, what am I doing well vs. not?
The good stuff: Similar to when I'm living from the creative level of consciousness. Present, listening, coaching, celebrating.
Areas to improve: Same as above – release concern about others' opinions, needing to be liked, and control (that will be a tough one).

Musings
I started asking some women in my networking group how they handle everything. This was hard; I didn't want to sound like I don't have my act together. Everyone laughed. Hardly anyone felt on top of things. That made me feel better. So we traded productivity hacks. Some have housecleaners and meal services where pre-portioned food shows up at your door with a recipe so you can make healthy, unprocessed food. I've never had either because of the expense, but I'm going to explore it.

One woman teaches productivity (who knew there was such a thing?). She asked how far ahead I plan. (My inside voice said, "Plan! Who has time to plan?") She plans a year ahead. My eyes bugged out. She shared her system. She has a one-pager with annual goals for work, kids, everything. She has four others with quarterly goals (three months per page). Then there's one page for each month and a weekly one. I was tired just thinking about it. But it makes sense. Because she looks at the whole year every week, nothing gets away from her. She delegates things that aren't due until the next quarter. Wow.

My biggest aha: my lack of planning. I suck at delegating because I handle things at the last minute. It's not fair to my staff to dump big deliverables on them without much turnaround time.

Galvanize	Galvanize: get excited into taking action

I don't feel shocked and excited into action. It's more like a slow burn. I can't sustain how I'm living. I don't want to feel stressed out and like nothing I ever do is enough. I felt a great burst of energy when I embarked on this process and I was convinced that I could fix it, but now I'm not so sure I can change anything.

KELLIE GARRETT

Obstacles	Obstacles that may get in your way: internal and external

There are so many obstacles, I don't know where to start.
My Never Good Enough Dragon.
My job: it's demanding and senior and my peers are performing just fine, so how can I stop doing anything? I'll look like I can't cut it. And maybe I can't but I don't want them to know that. I'll feel like a failure.
The kids: I feel guilty that work takes up so much time. When I'm home, I feel like I can't do anything other than cater to them.
The house: my partner doesn't pull his weight and all the nagging in the world hasn't changed anything. I'm at my wit's end and I don't know what to do.

What's preventing you from the desired future state?
I can't get everything done at work. There aren't enough hours in the day.
My attachment to being liked and in control.

New	New way of being, behaving, and believing

Hire a housecleaner.
Set 30 minutes aside every Sunday to plan my week/month/quarter. Put big tasks in my calendar. Feels daunting but I'll try it.
Figure out what can be hot-dog quality versus steak and lobster.
Talk to my team about what they think I should stop doing.
Come up with a mantra to deal with Never Good Enough Dragon.

Self	Continuous alignment between your higher self and your words and actions

I'm going to try one of the practices to connect with my higher self. Walking appeals to me most.
I will journal to my higher self, asking what she wants me to know. Not sure how that will work but again, I'm willing to try.

Summary:

			Dragon	Thinking	Feelings/Body	Wisdom from HigherSelf
D	Different	What I want to be different	Never Good Enough	Balance in my life	Hopeful	You can do this!
R	Reality	Current state	Dragon drives insecurity	I work 55+ hours a week	Stressed, anxious; Guilty about time away from kids; Body is tight, unhealthy from no exercise	How is this serving you, dear one?

SELF-COACHING THE DRAGON WITHIN

			Dragon	Thinking	Feelings/ Body	Wisdom from HigherSelf
A	Awareness & Aha's	Patterns, etc.	Insecurity drives overwork, perfectionism	I lack boundaries; people pleasing gets in way. I don't plan enough.	Defeated	This circumstance isn't permanent. Allow yourself to feel what you feel.
G	Galvanize	Feel shocked or excited into action: motivated to change	Dragon is making me not trust that I can do this	I don't feel moved to action. I do feel motivated to change.	I feel dumb for not knowing how to fix my situation.	That's funny! You certainly aren't dumb.
O	Obstacles	What might prevent you from making changes?	Dragon: "You know you can't do this. If you don't produce top-quality work, you'll get fired."	Big exec job: Where can I cut back hours? Failing to meet deadlines.	Feeling hopeless. It's no use.	It's okay to feel daunted. Know that your dragon is wrong and you will conquer the balance issue.
N	New	New way of being/ reacting	Need to find a way to lessen the dragon's power	Planning; Select what quality things need to be; Delegate/ stop some work	Cautiously optimistic	It's okay to feel daunted. Know that your dragon is wrong and you will conquer the balance issue.
S	Self/soul	Constant re-alignment with higher self/ soul	Dragon is obscuring my higher self	I've had glimpses of my higher self but I'm not sure I can consistently summon her.	Hesitant	Don't worry. Connection with me will come when you least expect it. Choose a practice and stick to it.

CHAPTER 16 WORKBOOK

Your turn! Choose an issue to coach yourself about and use this template to walk yourself through the process. Choose an issue you want to explore with self-coaching. It may be one of those covered in Chapters 7–13:

- Self-awareness and self-management (emotional intelligence)
- Trust building and rebuilding
- Confidence
- Mental toughness
- Political savvy, power, and ethical influence
- Giving and receiving hard feedback

You can use the questions contained in the table on the next page and/or the additional ones in the Appendix. Or you can come up with some of your own. ☺

You can download this table on my website: kelliegarrett.ca

SELF-COACHING THE DRAGON WITHIN

		Questions	Answers from my thoughts	What my feelings/body's telling me	What my Higher Self is telling me
D	Different: What I want to be different Dragons holding me back	What do I want to be different? When things are different, what will that future state look like? What concerns me? What's holding me back? What are the benefits of changing? What do I need to do differently to enhance my leadership? What feeds my soul? What gives me energy? What drains it? How does this dragon drive my behavior? Does my higher self have any guidance on my desired future state, dragon, or goal?			
R	Reality: Outline your current situation	What's my part to play in what's happening? What patterns can I identify in my beliefs, behaviors, and reactions? Can I detect a theme in things that are causing me stress? What's working about the current situation? What's not working about staying where I am? Does my higher self have any guidance regarding my current reality?			
A	Awareness What part do you have to play in the current reality? What patterns are you exhibiting? & Aha's	What's my part to play in what's happening? What patterns can I identify in my beliefs, behaviors, and reactions? What's my life lesson? (Something difficult that keeps showing up with a lesson to learn) When I'm at my best, what am I like? When I'm at my worst, what am I like? What circumstances do I view as unchangeable? Why? How might I deal with what I truly cannot change? What level of consciousness do I operate from? Where would I like to be? Do I have an attachment to being smart, liked, or in control? If so, how can I release this attachment? If I were to view leadership as a way of being, what am I doing well vs. not? Does my higher self have anything to add regarding my self-awareness exploration?			

KELLIE GARRETT

		Questions	Answers from my Thoughts	What my feelings/ body's telling me	What my Higher Self is telling me
G	Galvanize: Moved to action and motivated to change. How will you sustain this feeling? What will you do to act on what you know now?	What excites me about reaching my goal? How will I sustain my motivation? If I've tried before without success, what is different this time? When I experience a setback, how do I talk to myself? What will I do when I feel discouraged to stay the course?			
O	Obstacles What might prevent you from making the changes?	What is the biggest thing that may prevent me from reaching my goal? What other obstacles do I expect to encounter? What prevents me from living from a higher state of consciousness? What stops me from manifesting leadership as a way of being? How might my dragon(s) stand in the way of reaching my goal? What strategies do I need to combat my dragon? Are there ways I self-sabotage beyond what my dragon does? How do I get in my own way now and how might I get in my own way in the future? How might I surmount these obstacles? When I experience a setback or major challenges, what's my typical reaction?			
N	New New way of being/ reacting	Where do I want to be a year from now with respect to my goal? What do I need to get there? (e.g., beliefs, behaviors) What are my next steps? What's one action I can take to move me toward my goal? Capabilities: Do I know how to do this new thing? If not, can I outline what skills I need to support my ability to change? What practices will I adopt to support my new way of being, behaving, and believing? What kind of support will help me? How will I stay accountable to myself? What does my higher self have to say?			

SELF-COACHING THE DRAGON WITHIN

		Questions	Answers from my Thoughts	What my feelings/ body's telling me	What my Higher Self is telling me
S	Higher self: Constant re-alignment with higher self/soul	Now that I've completed all this, what does my higher self have for me in terms of guidance?			

Once you've completed the above, create a summary chart:

			Dragon	Thinking	Feelings/ Body	Wisdom from HigherSelf
D	Different	What I want to be different				
R	Reality	Current state				
A	Awareness & Aha's	Patterns, etc.				
G	Galvanize	Feel shocked or excited into action: motivated to change				
O	Obstacles	What might prevent you from making changes?				
N	New	New way of being/reacting				
S	Self/ soul	Constant re-alignment with higher self/soul				

You can use the DRAGONS self-coaching model for big existential issues or smaller things that you want to change. There are templates available on my website at https://kelliegarrett.ca.

PART V

THE JOURNEY TO MASTERY

CHAPTER 17: SELF-MASTERY AND TRANSCENDENCE

You've learned about leadership as a way of being, levels of consciousness, your higher self, common coaching issues, and the DRAGONS self-coaching model. These will help your journey to self-mastery. It's time to embark on a journey of transcendence—going beyond yourself to show up enlightened, to fail, and to rise again—committed to making a difference in the world.

> "WITHOUT SELF-MASTERY, WE ARE SLAVES TO FEAR, IMPULSE AND CONFORMITY. WITH SELF-MASTERY, JOY, GREATNESS AND TRANSCENDENCE ARE OURS."
>
> –Brendon Burchard[48]

Leadership mastery requires self-mastery, which isn't for the faint of heart. That's why I chose the subtitle *The hardest person you'll ever lead is you.* Diminishing the power of your dragons within is key. Their fire-breathing ways cloud self-awareness and a connection to your higher self. When the smoke clears, moving up the vertical development ladder will be easier (not easy).

If you truly want to be the best you possible, accept that you're human. No matter how conscious you become, you'll still be imperfect. You'll overreact, cry over a slight or a friend's insensitivity, or ignore your partner's bid for affection. (After decades of self-improvement, it's annoying that I'm still . . . human.)

Author Paul Weinfield writes, "In the real hero's journey, the dragon slays YOU. Much to your surprise, you couldn't make that marriage work . . . you turned forty with no kids, no house, and no prospects . . . the world didn't want the gifts you proudly offered it." He goes on to say that the foolish abort the journey and keep trying others. The wise feel a shattering and humility, releasing the need for winning and recognition. He urges us to view dragons as angels: "This is where your transcendent life begins."[49]

Striving for higher consciousness isn't about becoming Yoda or Buddha. But that doesn't get you off the hook. The other trap for the upwardly mobile on the higher consciousness front is smugness. I have more equanimity than you. I am perfection itself. Not. Apparently, when asked about his weaknesses, the Dalai Lama rattled them off. He was completely fine with his flaws. The interviewer asked why. He laughed and said being human comes with issues.

Acknowledging your weaknesses isn't weakness. It allows you to be unfazed when you notice them or someone else points them out. You'll be curious about ideas others have about how you can improve. Paradoxically, when you're familiar with your weaknesses, you become much less reactive. This allows you to listen to and even welcome others' criticism. You can decide whether their perspectives have merit. This enhances how you operate. It's impressive to watch someone receive feedback with curiosity rather than defensiveness. When you've done your inner work, defensiveness simply isn't there. Your mind is open to other perspectives because it isn't preoccupied with protecting itself.

I had the misconception that operating from this place meant that I wouldn't react anymore. As a champion self-criticizer (hello, Perfecto), I still fight a feeling of failure when I react. I simultaneously need to be kind to myself (Oh, honey, that hurt!) and tough (Okay, Garrett, enough sniveling. Dust yourself off, figure out your part to play, and learn from it!).

Sometimes I feel incapable of reaching the next level of consciousness—until I suddenly do. My perspective changes or I feel more open. I clearly see what I couldn't see before, so I wonder what else I don't see. Until I get trapped again by something else. Evolving from one level to another isn't like climbing stairs. You don't get to the next floor and stay there. You don't even get to keep the map: it keeps changing. The path forward vanishes. It's about feeling your way forward.

So, if it's a constant journey and the destination is never reached, why bother? Great question. It's a choice. But for some of us, it doesn't feel like a choice. It's a persistent calling . . . *there's more . . . you're getting there . . . it will be an amazing vista . . . you'll have more of that elusive inner peace . . . you can contribute to making the world a better place and encourage others to do that too . . .*

Elevating consciousness to reach transcendence

The very few who ascend to the unitive levels of development are often sages or spiritual leaders. The world is experienced as oneness with life itself. Universal compassion is the result: you feel connected to everything and everyone. Transcendence, the level below, is similar, with a major focus on "we."

At the end of his life, Abraham Maslow pondered moving beyond self-actualization ("me" focus) to transcendence: "Transcending one's self and finding one's unique purpose that best helps others . . . we go beyond the self . . . experiencing a radical shift in perspective, including a communion beyond the boundaries of the self."[50] Scott Barry Kaufman built on Maslow's unfinished work in his book *Transcend*. Kaufman argues that "healthy transcendence involves harnessing all that you are in the service of realizing the best version of yourself so you can help raise the bar for the whole of humanity."[51] How wonderful is that? We strive to be the best we can be, which helps everyone.

Operating from this place moves you to make a difference beyond yourself. To translate this loftiness to the business world, there's no need to put a corporate hat on because you think beyond your silo. You consider your organization's external context and its impact on the community and beyond. In your personal life, you care about the well-being of your family, friends, and even strangers. How amazing life would be if we all had this mindset.

Remember the levels of consciousness diagram in Chapter 2? The more elevated your consciousness, the more you understand you're part of something greater. That may be a connection to all of humanity, to nature, your concept of God, or the universe. Leadership as a way of being requires this connection to something larger than yourself. When you have practices that help you access this connection, you're more apt to keep things in perspective, grant yourself grace when (not if) you screw up, and extend that grace to others.

This is the route to using your gifts to make a difference in the world.

This isn't to be confused with spiritual bypassing, which is about avoiding difficult feelings by replacing them with toxic positivity. Painful emotions are normal, such as grief, anger, or anxiety. When you lose someone, you shouldn't suppress grief. When you're angry, a boundary may have been crossed. You need to act on the feeling without acting out. When you're anxious, you might need help. These are healthy responses. Your dragons don't disappear even if you live your life from a place of elevated consciousness. In fact, dragons are amazing accomplices in growing your wisdom and connecting with all that is.

Your level of consciousness can even contribute to world peace

When I was five, I drew a windmill and my mother ripped it up, saying it was a swastika. She told me about the Holocaust. The idea that people kill other people blew my little mind. I've been captivated by world peace ever since. I'm writing this after visiting Nagasaki. Viewing pictures of incinerated bodies and the city's complete destruction resulted in a horrified, holy silence. We know about the famous wars of history. But bloody conflicts still exist, ending countless lives lost and bringing untold suffering for survivors. The world desperately needs all of us to operate from a place of transcendence: concern for the whole.

A related concept is from Catherine O'Brien, who developed the concept of sustainable happiness. She defines this as "happiness that contributes to individual, community, and/or global well-being without exploiting other people, the environment or future generations."[52] This makes a link between well-being, happiness, and sustainability.[53] What if we all paid attention to living like this? It would improve your own life and benefit others well beyond your circle and even the planet. In your own life, you will be contributing to world peace and sustainability. You owe it to your fellow human beings to work on elevating your consciousness every day.

Awe: the ticket to transcendence

One of the ways to experience transcendence is by noticing, and even seeking, moments of awe. I saw a very young baby today and felt it. Such a miracle, this new being, looking at everything in wide-eyed wonder. I also saw a wild hare. He looked at me with big soulful eyes for a long time before he bounded away. Time stopped.

> *"THAT FEELING—OF BEING IN THE PRESENCE OF SOMETHING VAST THAT TRANSCENDS YOUR UNDERSTANDING OF THE WORLD— IS GOOD FOR US . . . IT CAN OFTEN BE FOUND IN COMPLETELY UNREMARKABLE CIRCUMSTANCES."*
> –Dacher Keltner, author of *Awe*[54]

Keltner says that awe occurs in daily moments: "a friend's generosity, a leafy tree's play of light and shadow on a sidewalk, a song that transported them back to a first love." And awe also occurs when you witness kindness, people standing up to bullies at work, or reading an inspiring book. On top of that, awe is a natural stress reliever and benefits you physically. Even better, awe sparks self-transcendence, which can result in greater wisdom and make us "more inclined to take others' perspectives, have humility, and be more empathetic."[55]

Some of the thoughts on how to access your higher self in Chapter 3 may be helpful gateways to connect with the spiritual and invite transcendence. Whatever you choose and however you seek to manifest higher consciousness, remember that leadership is a way of being. It's a choice every single day.

My wish for you

I called this book *Self-Coaching the Dragon Within* because I've witnessed the power of doing so with countless coaching clients as well as myself. Being a great leader is about a way of being—being a great human. And the word "human" says it all: flawed, vulnerable, imperfect, requiring connection—alive in our messiness.

I hope you have some useful nuggets to help you coach yourself. Coaching is about getting you from the current state to a desired future state. Coaches provide a safe place to bare it all and bear it, simultaneously holding your feet to the fire so you can reach your goal. The magic of transformation only works when we stop externalizing blame and stop internalizing it (it's all my fault). The more you realize how consistently imperfect you are, the more compassion you'll have for yourself and others' imperfections. The less likely you think you have all the answers, the better others will think of you. It's a fine virtuous spiral. Eventually, you can coach yourself to a space of elevated consciousness, again and again. But it won't be easy, dealing with your dragons within. The hardest person you'll ever lead is you.

How you choose to lead your life flows from how you choose to lead yourself. Do you listen to your higher self? Do you transcend selfish needs and wants while still looking after yourself? Think about expanding your sense of leadership to how you "be" everywhere in your life:

- Collaborating with colleagues and not talking behind anyone's back
- With your partner
- Co-parenting with your ex, putting your children first, and not criticizing their other parent
- Being fully present with your children
- Giving yourself what you want from others: compassion
- Making a difference everywhere you wander

I hope you've gleaned some ideas that will help you coach yourself and enhance how you lead and how you live. The world needs your leadership.

Trust yourself.

> "WE CONTRIBUTE TO ONE ANOTHER. WHATEVER OUR PURPOSE IS, WHEN WE TAKE ACTIONS WITH THAT PURPOSE, WE CAUSE TRANSFORMATION. WE ARE INTERCONNECTED TO EACH OTHER, AND THE DEEPER CONNECTIONS WE NURTURE, THE MORE IMPACT WE HAVE."
>
> –Sky Nelson-Isaacs, physicist, speaker, author, musician

EPILOGUE – THIS IS YOUR HIGHER SELF SPEAKING

"The soul's high adventure is to slay the dragon."
–Joseph Campbell, mythologist

In the prologue, I asked you to pretend your higher self is a coach who sits in complete non-judgment. A safe sounding board. A source of inner wisdom. A still place that already knows how amazing you are.

And you did it! You derive great strength from this connection. Your growth in self-awareness and its pesky cousin self-management are improving how you talk to yourself. Your commitment to growing your level of consciousness is yielding results. You really are manifesting leadership as a way of being. You've had the courage to identify the dragons within. You see how they're related to your towering strengths and crippling flaws. You haven't been able to eradicate them completely but you're in the driver's seat. When they roar into view, you're not taken off guard. You have strategies to firmly deal with them. You can even laugh at some dragons. They're annoyingly predictable.

You know how to use the DRAGONS coaching process to set a goal and see it through. You can use it anytime—for things big and small. You have practices to still your mind and simply listen to your higher self. The hardest person you'll ever lead isn't you anymore.

My secret's out. Now you know: there's no separation between me and you. I AM you. We're fully integrated. How wonderful is that? From this place, how will you live into leadership? How will you make a difference—to everyone you love, work with, parent, and befriend? What will you contribute to the world?

How will you elevate your consciousness? The world is waiting.

> *"MASTERING YOURSELF IS TRUE POWER."*
> —LAO TZU

To view Bonnie Chapman's painting
Awakening Hope:

> *"WE ARE ALL ON A PATH OF TRANSFORMATIVE HEALING AND GROWTH, EMBRACING FORTITUDE TO WEATHER LIFE'S UNCERTAINTIES,*
> *CHOOSING FAITH OVER FEAR, AND HEALING OVER WOUNDEDNESS.*
> *BEING WILLING TO SHOW UP FOR OUR OWN HEARTS*
> *WITH VULNERABILITY, COURAGE, AND OPENNESS,*
> *WE ARE AWAKENING HOPE WITHIN."*
> —Bonnie Chapman, artist

PART VI
INTEGRATING YOUR LEARNINGS

MY LEARNING INTEGRATION PLAN

Bravo! You've made it through the book. At the end of every good training course, the facilitator asks you to ponder your learnings and plan how you'll integrate them with your life going forward. So that's your task now...

Look at the workbook section of every chapter and your journal. Use these as input to create your integration plan. (A fillable pdf is available at http://kelliegarrett.ca).

MY ACTION PLAN FOR SELF-COACHING
LEADERSHIP AS A WAY OF BEING
This is what leadership as a way of being means to me:
I am good at these leadership behaviors and will continue demonstrating them:
At work:
At home:
I want to grow my ability to demonstrate the following leadership behaviors:
At work:
At home:
What might get in the way and how will I address these obstacles?

ELEVATING MY CONSCIOUSNESS

Vis-à-vis the Universal Model of Leadership diagram (see Chapter 2), I primarily operate at the ____ level.

How I will benefit from raising my level of consciousness:

Raising my consciousness will enhance how I show up as a leader in these ways:
At work:

At home:

How will others benefit from elevating my level of consciousness?

To raise my level of consciousness, I will pursue the following (list practices, learning, habits, etc.):

Optional: access the free self-assessment at **https://leadershipcircle.com/free-self-assessment/** to discover where you land on the universal model of leadership. Note: Keep in mind that this is a self-assessment and therefore will only be as accurate as your level of self-awareness. Consider participating in the 360 version.

ACCESSING MY HIGHER SELF

What I think of the idea of an inner source of wisdom—my higher self:

Practices I will use (or already use) to tune into my higher self (see Chapter 3 and Appendix for ideas):

MY DRAGONS

The critical voices in my head say the following:

My voices fall under the following theme(s):
(In my case, it's usually related to not being enough—good enough, smart enough, etc.)

The name I've assigned to this dragon:

The belief that fuels this dragon:
(If it's Not Enough Dragon, the belief might be that you're stupid or you don't belong.)

Behaviors I demonstrate when in the dragon's grip:
(In my case, the Not Good Enough Dragon drove perfectionism.)

How this dragon holds me back:
How this dragon has served me:

Critical voices	Limiting belief	Behaviors	Dragon's name	What I need to do to combat this dragon

My observations about what I need to do going forward, having completed my DRAGONS model:

Mastery

How will I increase my ability to notice awe? (This may be a daily diary.)

How might incorporating awe into my days enrich my life?

How will I connect with my higher self as a gateway to awe?

Now, write your commitment to manifest leadership as a way of being, to connecting consistently with your higher self, and to continue to elevate your level of consciousness:

You did it! Yay for you! ☺

APPENDIX

Additional Coaching Questions

It may be useful to check out some of the coaching questions listed here. At the same time, don't worry about having the perfect questions. Remember Rilke: "Learn to love the questions themselves."

Kellie's favorite coaching questions

In addition to what's included in the DRAGONS model in Chapter 16, and in the workbooks at the end of each chapter, here are some of my favorite questions.

Life purpose / Goals

- Do you have a sense of what you'd like to do with your life? What dragons are preventing you from going for it?
- If money were no object, what would you change about your life/career?
- When you find yourself in the zone or in a state of flow, what are you doing, thinking, and feeling?
- What's happening right now that's making you want to change it?

Identity / Way of being

- Ponder your various identities. Which ones feel authentic? Which ones are driven by a dragon? (In my case, performer and philosophizer feel authentic; affection seeker is driven by Never Enough Dragon.)

- What do you love about yourself? What do you wish you could remove from yourself? Are these somehow related?
- What are your go-to thoughts and feelings?

Soul

- What feeds your soul?
- What drains your energy?
- Do you feel connected to your higher self—your inner compass?
- What practices do you have to connect you to your higher self?
- What practices do you have to foster calm and inner peace?
- What's your life lesson? (Something difficult that keeps showing up with a lesson to learn.)

Leadership

- What does leadership mean to you, at work and in your personal life? Are there similarities between the two?
- Are you living into leadership behaviors at work and home?
- Think of leaders who inspired you. How did they inspire you? (e.g., What did they do and not do?) Can you notice a theme that applies to these leaders?
- Think of leaders you don't want to emulate. Why? What did they do and not do?

Outcome oriented

- How do you want this to turn out?
- What do you want a year from now?
- What is your desired outcome?
- What benefits would you like to see?
- What's your plan?

Specific situations/issues

- If you could do anything without repercussion, how would you handle this situation?
- If you were willing to make this as easy as possible, what would you do? What would you not do? (Adapted from Lou Tice, former CEO of the Pacific Institute)
- Pretend that you're listening to a friend. What questions would you ask? What would you remind them of? What advice would you give?

Choosing what to improve

- What are your gifts?
- Is the area you want to improve an overplayed strength?
- What do your biggest supporters say you need to improve?
- What would one of your Darth Vaders (people who aren't your fans or downright dislike you) say you need to improve?
- Do the Darth Vaders and your fans have any feedback in common?

Values

- What would your closest friends and family members say is most important to you?
- You said you don't know why this is upsetting you so much. Is this crossing a value? (e.g., anger over unfairness where fairness is a value)

Feeling stuck

- How is this way of being serving you?
- When you experience a setback or major challenges, how would you describe your typical reaction?
- What have you tried so far?
- If you believed that everything would work out fine in the end, how would this alter things?
- How are others contributing to your current reality?
- What's your part to play in what's not working?
- What's your habitual reaction to the current situation?
- What have you tried so far?

Action steps / Accountability

- What will you have to do to stick to your plan?
- What are your next steps?
- When will you do it?
- How will you keep yourself on track?
- What support do you need?

Tracey Burns, Master Certified Coach

"My favorite question is the one that arrives as if by magic, abruptly and wondrously opening up a world previously unknown to the client. It's the closest I come to what [spiritual teacher] Michael Beckwith describes as 'through me.'"

Master Certified Coach Marcia Reynolds's favorite question when a client is stuck

Dr. Marcia Reynolds is a world-renowned coach and author. In an interview with coach Michael Bungay Stanier, Marcia said, "I always tell coaches your questions have to come out of the moment but there's one question that seems to work when people are stuck." She asks them to think five years out and what their biggest regret will be about something they didn't do. She then probes further, asking the client to ponder the future: "if you were looking back and had to choose one path over another, which one would you regret not doing . . . it's always amazing because they immediately know. So all of a sudden, it's clear."[56]

Susan Mann, Professional Certified Coach: Coaching Questions for Life and Career Transition

- What's calling you forward: in life, in your career? What are you yearning for?

- What do you stand for: your purpose, top values, key principles?
- Where do you see your actions most in alignment with your top values, least in alignment? What do you take from that?
- How do you want to be seen by others? What do you want to be known for?
- What are your big passions and aspirational goals?
- Which people are most important to you: who you're with; where you feel you belong?
- How do you want to make a difference, to contribute? What gives you a sense of meaning?
- What is your learning / growth edge? How do you want to develop as a human?
- If anything were possible, what would be the next high point on your lifeline?
- What is lifegiving and energizing to you?
- What are the commitments that matter most to you?
- What are your "bucket list" dreams? Are there any actions, big or small, you want to take soon to move you toward achieving one of them?
- How do you want your days and weeks to feel? How will you spend your time?
- What are the top talents, strengths, and skills you possess and that you love using?

Leslie Rohonczy, Executive Coach and Leadership Development Consultant at Leslie Rohonczy Consulting

- May I meet the inner critic in you? Can you please lend her/him your voice for a minute? What does she/he tell you, and in what tone?
- How is this serving you?
- If you *did* know, what *might* it be? (When someone says, "I don't know why it makes me uncomfortable," it takes the pressure off getting the "right" answer.)
- What compassionate message do you most need to hear in this moment?
- We're used to many types of "performance metrics" in our lives, but what are your "trust metrics": that you look for from others, and that you send out to others?
- When you made that commitment, which "self" (or version of you) actually made the commitment? (The performative, the instinctive, or the integrated you / the "current" you or the "aspirational" you.)
- What does your body know about this—from the perspective of your gut? From your heart? From your head?
- What's the truest, most beautiful story you can imagine about your career? Not the easiest or happiest ... what is the truest and most beautiful story? (This engages the storyteller and disengages the excuse maker.)
- Thinking about your aspirational future state, what system of daily habits will help this future version of you to exist?
- What's driving your striving?
- What are you grateful for *because* of this situation?

Diana Ward, Mastery Coach and Storyteller at ATB Wealth

- What resonates with you?
- How could you be wrong?
- What don't you know?
- What is another perspective?
- What could you be missing?
- What's one baby step you could take?
- What are you noticing?
- What's important to you about this?
- What meaning are you giving that?
- What is the gift in this?
- What is the learning in this?
- Where is this pointing you or what's this telling you?

Michael Bungay Stanier: The 7 Essential Coaching Questions[57]

- What's on your mind?
- And what else?
- What's the real challenge here for you?
- What do you want?
- How can I help?
- If you're saying yes to this, what are you saying no to?
- What was most useful for you?

Additional ideas to access your higher self

Meditation

Free resources at Harvard University's Stress and Development Lab: https://sdlab.fas.harvard.edu/mindfulness-acceptance-and-non-judgment

Journaling

The Lynda Barry Four-Square method involves drawing four squares, labeling them, and then completing the journaling very quickly: two minutes or less for each square.

DID Write down what you did that day	SAW Write what you saw or noticed
HEARD Write about what you heard—conversations, etc.	DRAWN Draw a quick sketch

Easy Body Recalibration

This practice was developed by Jodi Woollam, one of my former coaches. It includes elements of Jeffery Allen's work:

Sitting in a steady chair with both feet flat on the floor, gaze in front of you and let your eye gently rest on a point. (Allow the chair and the ground to do the work to hold your body so you can relax.) Breathe. Bring your awareness behind your eyes and on an exhale, close your eyes. Notice that your awareness is still behind your eyes and move it to the center of your head. Breathe normally, gently.

1) From the center of your head, notice the sensations of your body.

- Notice the assuredness of your feet on the floor and your buttocks on the chair.
- Notice areas in your body where there may be tension. For example, scan your back and spine, your belly, your shoulders, your jaw.
- Notice the specific sensations in these areas of your body (i.e., is there tightness, heat, pain, holding, or bracing?)
- Mindfully (with a gentle inhale and extended exhale) breathe light and invite ease and space into each of these areas.

Continue to breathe normally, gently.

2) From the center of your head, call back to you all the energy and attention that you have sent out to others, projects, or concerns from the past and the future.

- Feel the warmth and nurturance in your body and mind as your energy returns to you. Allow yourself to feel recentered and grounded. Inhale. Exhale.
- Bring to your mind's eye the point that was across from you. Hold your awareness behind your eyes. Breathe. When you're ready, open your eyes.
- Thank yourself for taking the time to recalibrate. Smile. Rise slowly and go on with your day.

END NOTES

1. Huntington, Charlie and Dr. Tchiki Davis. "How to Do Shadow Work," *Psychology Today,* November 20, 2023. https://www.psychologytoday.com/ca/blog/click-here-for-happiness/202308/how-to-do-shadow-work

2. Dethmer, Jim, Diana Chapman & Kaley Warner Klemp. *The 15 Commitments of Conscious Leadership: A New Paradigm for Sustainable Success.* (2015)

3. Excerpt from *The Charge of the Goddess,* credited to Doreen Valiente

4. Anderson, Bob. *Leadership Circle and Organizational Performance.* https://leadershipcircle.com/wp-content/uploads/2018/03/The-Leadership-Circle-and-Organizational-Performance.pdf

5. The theory base for the Leadership Circle Profile™ includes work by Peter Block – authenticity; Robert Burns – cognitive psychology; Center for Creative Leadership/DDI – competency research; Robert Fritz – creative orientation; Karen Horney – character structure; Carl Jung – ego/shadow; Robert Kegan – adult development; Abraham Maslow – self-actualization; David McLelland – achievement orientation; OSU – Task/relationship; Peter Senge – systems thinking.

6. Kegan, Robert. *In Over Our Heads.* (Harvard University Press, 1998)

7. Approved for publication by Robert J. Anderson, personal communication, April 5, 2024.

8. Anderson, Robert J. & William A. Adams. *Mastering Leadership.* (Wiley, 2015)

9. Mallel (Morad), Natalie. *Part 3: How to Be an Adult – Kegan's Theory of Adult Development,* April 23, 2020. https://medium.com/@NataliMorad/part-3-how-to-be-an-adult-kegans-theory-of-adult-development-3ed9f2340f9f

10. Anderson, Robert J. & William A. Adams. *Mastering Leadership.* (Wiley, 2015)

11. Adapted from "What Is the Transformative Learning Theory," *WGU,* July 17, 2020. https://www.wgu.edu/blog/what-transformative-learning-theory2007.html

12. Cook-Greuter, Susanne R. *Nine Levels of Increasing Embrace in Ego Development: A Full-Spectrum Theory of Vertical Growth and Meaning Making.* Revised 2013.

13. Adib, Rabieh. *"Mastering Leadership:* Review of a must-read leadership book." February 24, 2023. https://www.shinecoachingbarcelona.com/en/mastering-leadership-book-review/

14. Anderson, Bob. *The Leadership Circle: A Brief History.* https://leadershipcircle.com/wp-content/uploads/2018/03/The-Leadership-Circle-A-Brief-History.pdf

15. Schwartz, Dr. Richard. "The Larger Self," *IFS Institute* https://ifs-institute.com/resources/articles/larger-self

16. "The Jungian Model of the Psyche" *Journal Psyche* https://journalpsyche.org/jungian-model-psyche/

17. Sørensen, Kenneth. *The Soul of Psychosynthesis.* (Kentaur, 2016)

18. Brach, Tara. "Uncover the Golden Budda Within You," *Lion's Roar*, April 24, 2024. https://www.lionsroar.com/the-golden-buddha-inside-you/

19. Fairyington, Stephanie. "Connecting to Your Higher Self Will Transform Your Life." *Oprah Daily,* February 23, 2022. https://www.oprahdaily.com/life/health/a38736167/how-to-connect-to-your-higher-self/

20. Everyday Mindfulness with Jon Kabat-Zinn https://www.mindful.org/everyday-mindfulness-with-jon-kabat-zinn/

21. Tara Mohr website: https://www.taramohr.com/pbbookmaterials1/

22. Instagram @elizabeth_gilbert_writer, October 24, 2019, https://www.instagram.com/p/B4AZgjjh-NL/?hl=en

23. Kross, Ethan. Chatter: *The Voice in Our Heads, Why It Matters, and How to Harness It.* (Crown, 2022)

24. Sørensen, Kenneth. *The Soul of Psychosynthesis.* (Kentaur, 2016)

25. Schwartz, Dr. Richard. "The Larger Self." *IFS Institute.* https://ifs-institute.com/resources/articles/larger-self

26. "Korn Ferry Study identifies leadership challenges being coached most often," April 3, 2015, https://www.kornferry.com/about-us/press/korn-ferry-study-identifies-leadership-challenges-being-coached-most-often

27. Anderson, Robert J. & William A. Adams. *Mastering Leadership.* (Wiley, 2015)

28. "The Core Leadership Skills You Need in Every Role," *Center for Creative Leadership,* May 24, 2023 https://www.ccl.org/articles/leading-effectively-articles/fundamental-4-core-leadership-skills-for-every-career-stage/

29. Brown, Brené. *Dare to Lead.* (Random House, 2018)

30. Eurich, Tasha. "What Self-Awareness Really Is (and How to Cultivate It)" *Harvard Business Review,* January 2, 2018. https://hbr.org/2018/01/what-self-awareness-really-is-and-how-to-cultivate-it

31. The Leadership Circle™ is the best 360 I've encountered. It provides rich data for exploring levels of consciousness and enhancing leadership effectiveness. There is also a free self-assessment.

32. Feltman, Charles. *The Thin Book of Trust: An Essential Primer for Building Trust at Work.* (2021)

33. Private communication with Charles Feltman, March 24, 2024.

34. Reina, Dennis S. and Michelle L. Reina. *Trust & Betrayal in the Workplace.* (Berrett-Koehler; 3rd edition, 2015)

35. "Confidence," *Psychology Today,* https://www.psychologytoday.com/ca/basics/confidence#:~:text=Confidence%20is%20a%20belief%20in,feeling%20secure%20in%20that%20knowledge Retrieved October 13, 2023

36. Lewis, Oliver. "Women more likely to suffer from imposter syndrome than men, according to research." *Independent,* April 7, 2023. https://www.independent.co.uk/life-style/women-imposter-syndrome-workplace-confidence-b2313770.html#

37. Clough, Peter, and Doug Strycharcyzk. *Developing Mental Toughness.* (Kogan Page; 2 edition, 2015). Emphasis added.

38. AQR International website: https://aqrinternational.co.uk/

39. Strycharczyk, Doug. "Mental Toughness and Emotional Intelligence." *AQR International,* April 19, 2021. https://aqrinternational.co.uk/mental-toughness-emotional-intelligence

40. Reardon, Kathleen Kelly. *The Secret Handshake: Mastering the Politics of the Business Inner Circle.* (Doubleday, 2002)

41. *Development and Validation of the Political Skill Inventory,* Florida State University Foundation. (2005)

42. Jarrett, Michael. "The Four Types of Organizational Politics." *Harvard Business Review,* April 24, 2017. https://hbr.org/2017/04/the-4-types-of-organizational-politics

43. Valcour, Monique. "Anyone Can Learn to Be a Better Leader." *Harvard Business Review,* November 4, 2020. https://hbr.org/2020/11/anyone-can-learn-to-be-a-better-leader

44. The "W" in GROW was originally "Will"; that is, "What will you do?" It has been adapted to stand for the "Way forward."

45. Parker, Palmer. *A Hidden Wholeness: The Journey Toward an Undivided Life*. (Jossey-Bass, 2009)

46. Reynolds, Dr. Marcia. "Coaching is about more than asking questions." *International Coaching Federation*, June 22, 2015 https://coachingfederation.org/blog/coaching-is-about-more-than-asking-questions

47. International Coaching Federation website: https://coachingfederation.org/about

48. Burchard, Brendon. *The Motivation Manifesto: 9 Declarations to Claim Your Personal Power.* (Hay House, 2014)

49. Weinfield, Paul. "Letting the Hero Die." *Science and Non-duality*, December 19, 2022. https://scienceandnonduality.com/article/letting-the-hero-die/

50. Kaufman, Dr. Scott Barry. "There Is No One Way to Live a Good Life," Blog. September 20, 2017. https://scottbarrykaufman.com/no-one-way-live-good-life/

51. Kaufman, Dr. Scott Barry. *Transcend: The New Science of Self-Actualization.* (TarcherPerigee, 2020)

52. O'Brien, Catherine. "Happiness and Sustainability Together at Last! Sustainable Happiness." *Canadian Journal of Education / Revue Canadienne de l'éducation 36, no. 4 (2013): 228–56.* http://www.jstor.org/stable/canajeducrevucan.36.4.228.

53. Ibid.

54. Keltner, Dacher. "The Quiet Profundity of Everyday Awe." *The Atlantic.* https://www.theatlantic.com/family/archive/2023/01/feeling-in-awe-take-walk-visual-art/672617/

55. Kim, Y., Nusbaum, H. C., & Yang, F. (2022). "Going beyond ourselves: the role of self-transcendent experiences in wisdom." Cognition and Emotion, 1-19.

56. Interview with Michael Bungay Stanier, "Dr. Marcia Reynolds' One Best Coaching Question," *The Coaching Habit*, November 20, 2017

57. Stanier, Michael Bungay. *The Coaching Habit.* (Page Two Books, 2019)

AUTHOR BIO

KELLIE GARRETT is a recovering executive who witnessed, and occasionally participated in, the games played by leaders at the upper echelons. After working with several executive coaches (and a therapist or two), she experienced dramatic shifts to how she led her life: at work and everywhere else. Kellie is passionate about helping others realize their potential by learning to manage their inner dragons.

Her goal is to inspire you to view leadership as a way of being—a set of behaviors that fosters trust and helps others shine—at work and at home. This requires understanding adult vertical development, which is all about growing your level of consciousness, moving from *me-me-me* to *we*.

Kellie speaks and consults on leadership, high performance, culture change, group dynamics, board governance, and business strategy. She coaches C-suite executives and works with senior teams to build and rebuild trust, engage in constructive conflict, and model the kind of collaboration they say they want in their organizations. A Certified Dare to Lead™ Facilitator, Kellie incorporates the marvelous teachings of Brené Brown in her work.

A former senior vice president at an agribusiness financial institution, Kellie was responsible for business strategy, the customer experience, marketing communication, and innovation. She has been honored as a Master Communicator and Fellow by the International Association of Business Communicators, Canada's 100 Most Powerful Women, Top 25 Women of Influence, and a Red Cross Humanitarian Award for autism advocacy. Kellie currently serves as a Board member at the Mental Health Commission of Canada and the Global Coaching Education Board of the International Coaching Federation.

When she's not battling dragons or working too much, Kellie loves philosophizing with her husband, family and friends, quaffing wine, flower-gardening, travel, and messing around with art.

fEMPOWER
PUBLICATIONS

fEMPOWER Publications Inc. is a boutique publishing house and community serving purpose-driven women in the pursuit of big dreams. We offer full-service book production and publication, thought-leadership development programs, and collaborative writing opportunities for females of all ages.

www.fempower.pub

@fempower.pub
@fempower.pub

Join the Author{ity} Membership

Made in the USA
Monee, IL
29 January 2025